THE ECONOMICS OF PARENTING

THE ECONOMICS OF PARENTING

HIS GIFT, Your Giving, and HIS INCREASE

Kathy Scott-Gurnell, MD

ELM HILL

A Division of
HarperCollins Christian Publishing

www.elmhillbooks.com

The Economics of Parenting
HIS GIFT, Your Giving, and HIS INCREASE

Published in Nashville, Tennessee, by Elm Hill, an imprint of Thomas Nelson. Elm Hill and Thomas Nelson are registered trademarks of HarperCollins Christian Publishing, Inc.

Elm Hill titles may be purchased in bulk for educational, business, fund-raising, or sales promotional use. For information, please e-mail SpecialMarkets@ ThomasNelson.com.

All Scripture quotations, unless otherwise indicated, are taken from the New American Standard Bible®. Copyright © 1960, 1962, 1963, 1968, 1971, 1972, 1973, 1975, 1977, 1995 by The Lockman Foundation. Used by permission. (www.Lockman.org)

Scripture quotations marked KJV are from the King James Version. Public domain.

Scripture quotations marked NIV are from the Holy Bible, New International Version®, NIV®. Copyright © 1973, 1978, 1984, 2011 by Biblica, Inc.® Used by permission of Zondervan. All rights reserved worldwide. www.Zondervan.com. The "NIV" and "New International Version" are trademarks registered in the United States Patent and Trademark Office by Biblica, Inc.®

Scripture quotations marked NKJV are from the New King James Version®. © 1982 by Thomas Nelson. Used by permission. All rights reserved.

Cover Design: Rochelle Scott
Logo Design: Rion C. Gurnell

Library of Congress Cataloging-in-Publication Data
Library of Congress Control Number: 2019937965

ISBN 978-1-400326051 (Paperback)
ISBN 978-1-400326068 (eBook)

HIS GIFT, Your Giving, and HIS INCREASE

MAY 1, 2019

FOREWORD

I am honored, humbled, and excited to write this foreword for my dear friend of thirty-seven years, Dr. Kathy Scott-Gurnell. We have come a long way from being two young college students at the University of Texas at Austin. It is amazing to me how God orchestrated and predestined this friendship from the start, when I first met you at the Alpha Kappa Alpha Delta Xi interest meeting in 1982. These few paragraphs that I have been charged to write is a reminder of how God has blessed and anointed our friendship and sister-hood. God knew we would need the continued support and encouragement of each other for this life journey while rearing and supporting our families (three children each plus our wonderful husbands).

As we have grown older as friends and sisters,

we have also matured spiritually and realized that God had a purpose for this friendship. We have laughed together, cried together, reared children into productive young adults together (only by God's grace), and even survived our conflicts with each other. But God continued this maturing relationship that has lasted all these years. I could write a book on our journey as friends, but I just want to take the time to say thank you for being that "big sister," especially after the loss of my parents and grandparents. I will never forget your kindness during the time of my grandmother's death during my college years and we had just met. When my youngest son Stefan was struggling in elementary school, you encouraged me to seek outside help and to work with the teachers to get him additional assistance. He graduated with a biochemistry degree and is now working at MD Anderson in the Immunotherapy Research Group and on his master's in public health. When I found out I had breast cancer, at first you were in shock, but then you immediately came back and said, "Wait…wrong response. Let's pray." I am now a ten-year breast cancer survivor (praise God!). These are just a few of life's memories that we have prayed over and gone through during our thirty-seven-year friendship, and I thank God that you were a part of the experience.

After years of saying you were going to write a book and publish it… Congratulations! You did it! And, well, it's about time (smile). You have always been gifted at writing, teaching, and speaking, and now this book gives you the opportunity to put it all together. *The Economics of Parenting* will truly be a blessing to other parents and grandparents based on your sound advice and experiences of raising your own children and being a child and adolescent psychiatrist. Children are truly blessings and gifts from God, and your book breaks down how we as parents and grandparents need to use "God's economy" on raising our children. In your book you stated that just as we strategize and plan with our finances for the future, we need to do the same with raising our children in order to receive the maximum return and profit on our investments. I am also reminded of a quote by Frederick Douglass that states, "It is easier to build strong children than to repair broken men." Your book discusses how we should be intentional of what we pour into the lives of our children so that they are successful and prosperous and not broken and bankrupt. I pray that this book will be a blessing to every parent and grandparent who reads it as they receive a massive return on their investment from the fruit of their labor—not only from their children, but their family legacy of the next generation.

You and Morris have been wonderful examples of the sacrifice, dedication, and love it takes to rear godly, successful children; you both should be very proud. You both have given of your time and talents to intentionally deposit nuggets of encouragement, love, prayer, and God's Word into not only the lives of your own family but also into the lives of others (including my own). God is truly pleased and will continue to smile on both of you.

As I conclude I am again reminded of another quote: "The power of words is that a life can be launched with as little as a single phrase, an uplifting word or an act of kindness. Think of the power we wield and the impact we can make if we become more intentional about encouraging our children. Our words are often the very thing that help create future dreams. And sometimes those dreams are to be just like us" (author unknown). *The*

Economics of Parenting is a book to remind us to continue to be intentional about praying, depositing the Word, and encouraging our children. We never know what God has for their futures as we watch them grow into the successful young adults He has called them to be.

May you, my dear friend, continue to work in God's spirit and in His ordained purpose for your life, and may your obedient response to God's will to step out and write this book be a blessing not only to others but also to your life.

By Toni Crawford

TABLE OF CONTENTS

PART III

PART IV

PART V

PART VI: THE FINAL WORD

Preface and Acknowledgement

M any people measure success by their positions, their possessions, and their pocketbooks. Solomon, the wisest and richest man who ever lived, said this is all vanity (Ecclesiastics 1:14)—a waste of our time and energy. Why? Because it is all so temporary. In the United States we live on average eighty to eighty-four years. Back in Genesis 5, although years may have been measured differently, men lived 800–900 years. The interesting thing is, neither of these life spans are even a dot in time when compared to eternity. We all have a greater purpose in life, a higher calling and assignments to finish, before we move on to eternity. It should be our goal to complete our earthly assignments in a timely manner so that our transition to eternity can be rewarding.

Lessons on gaining success are commonly documented in books, articles, and videos. God's formula, which I refer to as "God's economy," suggests we look at success differently.

As children, success was the farthest thing from our minds. We were all carefree as we grew and matured, because the burden was on our parents and elders to shape us and lead us in the right direction. Guess what? We are now the parents and grandparents. What we do, say, and teach our children directly or indirectly effect not only their success but ours as well. This book is written to encourage parents to plan and strategize the upbringing of their children just as they do with their finances, to maximize the returns. I am not an expert in economic studies, but I have discovered God's economy system and realized it can be used in all areas of our lives, including parenting.

I thank God for revealing His system to me. The initial part of the book will offer fail-proof tools for parents, guardians, and grandparents. The latter portion of the book includes personal lessons that God revealed to me as I completed this book.

I want to acknowledge my editing team of Elm Hill division of Harper Collins Christian Publishing for their dedication, timeliness and expertise during this process. A special thanks to my proofreading friends: Toni Crawford, Cheryl Creuzogt, Kim DeVaughn, and Juanessa Winkfield, your time and expertise were invaluable. I am grateful to my parents, the late Mary Lee and Floyd Scott, Sr. I view them as the best parents in the world, who purposefully equipped me for my life's journey. I am grateful for every young person who lived in my home throughout the years, especially Jermaine, Levi, Raushanah and Cheryl. Your being there brought substance and blessings to my family. I also want to acknowledge my siblings and sibling-cousins for our monthly prayer time, which has helped me to remain encouraged to complete this book, in honor of our family legacy.

Last but certainly not least, I thank my husband Morris for thirty-two years of marital bliss, and my three amazing children who are now young adults—Braylon (Krystal), Kassie, and Rion—for allowing me the privilege to parent you.

As you pick up this book and began to read, it

is my prayer that this journey will enlighten each of you beyond your imagination. I pray that the pages of this book will bring a new hope, a sustained joy and a thirst for righteousness to your family legacy. Thank you for taking this walk of faith with me.

PART I

This section describes God's Economy and how his scripture supports this concept. Amazingly, God's Economy can influence and shape every area of our lives, especially parenting. His system is perfect and offers success without question. Open your hearts to receive his master plan.

CHAPTER 1

THE THEOLOGY OF
GOD'S ECONOMICS

"God's economics are fail-proof."

—Dr. KSG

To understand where this book is taking us, we must look back to see where God's instructions have led us. Let's begin by discussing the title of this book, *The Economics of Parenting: HIS GIFT, Your Giving,* and *HIS INCREASE.* Is that not what we spend a lifetime to acquire: increase, wealth and success? The Lord reveals through His Word His system of growth and prosperity.

Step 1: Begins with Deuteronomy 6:2: "so that you and your son and your grandson might fear the

LORD your God, to keep all His statutes and His commandments which I command you, all the days of your life, and that your days may be prolonged." (NASB)

Here God tells us to live our lives in respect and love of Him by keeping His commandments. He goes a step further and says, not just you, but your sons and grandsons. This does not stop with one, two, or even four generations. If we are keeping his statutes "all of the days of our lives," we will influence many generations, and this is God's intention.

Step 2: Deuteronomy 28:1–6 remind us that if we make it our business to carefully and habitually obey His Word, He will give us blessings that will awe us and overtake us.

Deuteronomy 28:1–6 (NASB): *Now it shall be, if you diligently obey the LORD your God, being careful to do all His commandments which I command you today, the LORD your God will set you high above all the nations of the earth.*

All these blessings will come upon you and overtake you if you obey the LORD your God.

Blessed shall you be in the city and blessed shall you be in the country.

...Blessed shall be the offspring of your body and the produce of your ground and the offspring of your beasts, the increase of your herd and the young of your flock.

Blessed shall be your basket and your kneading bowl.

Blessed shall you be when you come in, and blessed shall you be when you go out.

These simple two steps, my friend, is what I call "God's economy." That is, we obey and He blesses bountifully. Wise men would call that success. OK, some of you are saying that is just a couple of scriptures. Well, He says this repeatedly throughout His Word. If you have ever studied Bible literature or God's Word, you know if something repeats, it is really, really important. Let me encourage you to now take the time to read a few more scriptures that essentially say the same thing. Scriptures like:

Malachi 3:10 (NASB): *"Bring the whole tithe into the storehouse, so that there may be food in My house, and test Me now in this,"* says *the Lord of hosts, "if I will not open for you the windows of heaven and pour out for you a blessing until it overflows."*

Matthew 6:33 (NKJV): *"But seek first the kingdom of God and His righteousness, and all these things shall be added to you."*

Luke 6:38 (NIV): *"Give, and it will be given to you. A good measure, pressed down, shaken together and running over, will be poured into your lap. For with the measure you use, it will be measured to you."*

God's economy is no joke; it is real. I have been a direct recipient of His promises, they are true. In my unsophisticated, limited search of God's Word for His economy, I discovered many scriptures that support His economy, both directly and indirectly. That is, there are as many scriptures stating that those who disobey God will suffer as there are scriptures that say those who obey will be blessed. (The entire book of Proverbs is dedicated to this truth.)

Plainly stated:

Obedience = permanent blessings and eternal life

Disobedience = transient/absent blessings and eternal death

Psalm 1 is another perfect example of scripture comparing the righteous from the unrighteous.

Psalm 1:1–6 (NASB): *"How blessed is the man who does not walk in the counsel of the wicked, nor stand in the path of sinners, nor sit in the seat of scoffers! But his delight is in the law of the LORD, And in His law he mediates day and night. He will be like a tree firmly planted by streams of water, Which yields its fruit in its season and its leaf does not wither; And in whatever he does, he prospers. The wicked are not so, But they are like chaff which the wind drives away. Therefore the wicked will not stand in the judgment, Nor sinners in the assembly of the righteous. For the LORD knows the way of the righteous, But the way of the wicked will perish."*

Another interesting thing about God and His economy is it does not just apply to money. God's economy crosses over to all areas of life, including spirituality and maturity. Remember how Jesus often told his disciples, "Assuredly, I say to you, whatever you bind on earth will be bound in heaven, and whatever you loose on earth will be loosed in heaven" Matthew 18:18 (NKJV). Again, another example of God's economic system revealed. Rather than trying to make things perfect and right for ourselves and our families using our own might and strength, God is asking us to let it go and allow Him to order our steps and assure our increase. Our God does everything decent and in order. His system is simple and inviting and extremely rewarding. Right now I am not at all talking about money. This is about life, decisions, relationships, beliefs, and actions. More specifically this book outlines God's economy as it relates to parenting.

It is my prayer that the following chapters will awaken your spiritual nurturing power. This power, influenced by God and directed by the Holy Spirit, will assure you deposit healthy investments and acquire massive returns, as you rear your children and grandchildren.

CHAPTER 2

TURNING AND RE-TURNING

"Man's economy (give and take) versus God's economy (give and give)."

—Dr. KSG

P arenting can be one of the most anxiety-producing, but exciting, experiences known to humans. I am the biological mother of three children and assisted with rearing numerous others. Allow me to reminisce on my pregnancy experiences. There is this strange but ecstatic feeling of having a little person growing inside of you. I remember the months when I could forget I was pregnant, with very little signs other than a protruding abdomen and no monthly girlfriend. I can also recall the months when I was so awkward that walking felt like a new balancing act. I think they call it "wobbling" (not the line dance), caused by the unequal distribution of your weight. Fast forward to the day of my firstborn's birth: I could not believe it! First, the unbelievable level of pain, which God allows a mother to forget the instant she lays eyes on her infant. John 16:21 (NASB): "Whenever a woman is in labor she has pain, because her hour has come; but when she gives birth to the child, she no longer remembers the anguish because of the joy that a child has been born into the world." Really, mothers, think about that; first, they call it "labor," but the physical exertion starts from conception. Labor is required to have a newly created human develop over nine months and then deliver them into this world. Next is the level of pain the young mother is exposed to, which feels impossible to endure. Yet the instant the baby is born a calmness appears that overshadows the pain, as if it dropped into the middle of the sea. Don't get me wrong, labor is painful, but only for a brief moment compared to the years of joy watching your child grow. I can't imagine or compare it to anything I have ever experienced.

It is indeed a once-in-a-lifetime occasion, with each birth. In Genesis 3:16 (NASB), God gave women a punishment for Eve's disobedience: "...I will greatly multiply your pain in childbirth, In pain you will bring forth children..." Therefore it is no accident that the pain is so great. God gives us the pain but turns around and gives us grace in the beautiful child who brings joy, overshadowing the pain. This is so God, giving and giving again. Just like the rainbow he promises after a great pouring of rain. If I may digress, this takes me to Christ's sacrifice on the cross. It, too, is a once-in-a-lifetime experience that, although I know it happened, I know it was painful, yet it can truly never occur again. Calvary requires no reruns. It was complete at that very moment, and it's results last throughout eternity. I call that God's amazing grace. Likewise I am grateful that my child's physical birth never has to be repeated. Back to the pain, I can try to remember the details of the pain of labor, but I really can't. I have heard other mothers try to describe it, but if you listen to the descriptions they offer, for example, "Like a bomb exploded in my body," which of course no human has lived to offer details. So I will just stick with John 16:21, God rescued our minds from the agony. At any rate, nothing, not even the pain, can compare to the extreme joy of seeing my healthy baby crying and frantically throwing his long legs and arms in the air, until I picked him up, swaddled him, and placed him as close to my heart as possible. OK, every mother reading this knows that is the moment when love has a new meaning. I can't stay here because my first son is now married, and I have relinquished the monopoly of all those mushy thoughts to his number one lady, his wife.

I feel qualified to write this book on parenting because I learned so much over the years as I diligently tried to rear each of the children God placed under our care, in the fear and admonition of the Lord. Truth be told I could not think of any other way to do it because I was truly scared to death. Fear drove me straight to a path of parenthood, which I believe paid off big time, and that is what I want to share with you.

The economics of parenting really evolved from my study of the scriptures and increasing understanding of God's will, God's way, and God's payoff. He tells us to do everything decent and in order, because that is his way (1 Corinthians 14:40). He is very loving, merciful, and systematic. His dividends are second to none; they are everlasting, never lacking.

Often when we think of God's economics we think of tithing. I will admit that is what I was studying when my "aha" moment came. You know the two most common scriptures, one Old Testament and the other New Testament, but both basically saying the same thing. Just in case you did not digest them when mentioned earlier:

Malachi 3:10 (NASB): ***"Bring the whole tithe into the storehouse, so that there may be food in My house, and test Me now in this,"*** says the L ORD of hosts, ***"if I will not open for you the windows of heaven and pour out for you a blessing until ᵈit overflows."***

Luke 6: 38 (NASB): ***"Give, and it will be given to you. They will pour into your lap a good measure—pressed down, shaken together, and running over. For by your standard of measure it will be measured to you in return."***

Scripture tells us everything belongs to God. He then graciously gives us a portion from which he expects us to return a much smaller portion, which he then returns to us multiplied in an even larger portion. I picture an exponential cycle and I will use this illustration with money, because that we all understand. God gives me $100.00. I in turn give him $10.00, with gratitude not a bad attitude. He then gives me $200.00 and I give him $20.00. He gives me $400.00 and I give him $40.00 with gratitude not a bad attitude, and so on and so forth. Simple, systematic, and sustaining, God's economics.

The Lord revealed that his economics does not just apply to money, but it can flow through many areas of our lives, ministries, careers, and yes, child-rearing. Regarding ministry, the more willing I am to serve others, the more opportunities to serve God gives. The more I use my job to give him glory, the more he blesses me to excel in my career. We have heard of a "give and take" relationship. We function well in this type of exchange. Our civilization operates based on this standard. I give you a service and you pay for it. I give you money and I open my hand for the item purchased. My God, however, works from a different standard, a heavenly standard. He tells us his ways are not our ways (Isaiah 55:8b). God does not operate on a give-and-take system. He operates on a "give and give" system. It is almost like, if we turn toward him, he will quickly lead us in the right path. He is willing to make our small steps gain more ground than humanly possible. It is with this system in mind that I reared my children.

I am not saying that I have perfect children by any means. As a matter of fact, after starting this chapter, God took me on a detour with my children. The enemy attacked and tried to discourage me from completing this book. I had not written in two months and did not understand why. During that two-month period, my daughter, then twenty-four years old, almost lost her virginity. What saved her was her love for God, the young man's obedience to God, and God's magnificent grace. Simultaneously my son appeared to be under persecution for telling the truth. The persecution appeared to be turning into a punishment. Fasting and praying as a family became a must. But for the goodness of God, righteousness prevailed, and I am still writing. So again I am not saying I am a perfect parent, or that I reared perfect children who are above the temptations of the world. But I am saying we do have the power of perfection available to us, from God's Word, by the example of our Savior Jesus Christ, and with the assistance of the Holy Spirit.

As another disclaimer, I am not saying I know all there is to know about parenting. I am not saying I always did the right thing or knew the right thing to do when it came to rearing children. What I will say is that I prayed and thought this thing out because I was so fearful. Only by the grace of a loving God has it worked to my advantage and to my children's advantage. Looking back, I realized that it is a testimony to God's economy in that godly parenting in a certain manner **turns** your children towards God and God will **turn** them toward the right path. So I guess you can say this is a book on **turning**. Just **turning**. Like riding a bicycle, steering a boat, driving a car, just **turning and re-turning**.

CHAPTER 3

YOU ARE YOUR BEGINNING

"A man's success is not measured by what he does or gains in life, but by the success of his children."

—Uncle Edward Gurnell

In this chapter, I want to share a story that helps differentiate between man's economics and God's economics. This story may help explain the process of maturation required before this book could become a reality. Pay close attention to the twist and turns of life that led to God's final product. My knowledge of God's economics started almost thirty years ago. My husband's great-uncle, a very wise man now in heaven, often greeted others by handing them a business card. Interestingly, as I remember it, the card was not to advertise a business; rather it had his contact information on one side and on the back side was a poem he wrote Entitled: "Measure of a Man". (see appendix) I was so intrigued by this unusual presentation of one's self that I ventured to have a conversation with Uncle Edward about the reason he gives the cards. Uncle Edward appeared to be somewhat of a storyteller and I was captivated by his wisdom. It turned out, his card was used as a catalyst to invite a conversation, which allowed him to share his story and, more importantly, the gospel. At the end of our conversation, which was rich with wisdom and knowledge, I summed it up in the quotation at the beginning of this chapter, which I will credit to Uncle Edward. "A man's success is not measured by what he does or gains in life, but by the success of his children." This pearl of wisdom really amazed and challenged me. At the time, I had one child and he was only about two months old. I honestly had given no thought to his success as a human being. Truthfully my only prayer for him was to survive my inexperience as a mother and make it to his first birthday. This explains why first birthday parties are more for the parents than the infant. I barely saw myself as a mother, but rather as a wife, a daughter, and, most importantly to me at the time, as a medical student. The latter was where I dreamt to be most of my life, and prior to hearing Uncle Edward's statement I thought that "I had arrived." The knowledge gained that day challenged my every purpose and existence. This was very humbling for me. I instantly began to look at my completion of medical school as a metaphor for something greater than myself. This medical degree could reward my parents for all the hard work they put in over the years to assure that my siblings and I were successful. This was my rationale for hyphenating my last name, to give tribute to the Scott legacy. Likewise, the same medical degree would be a catalyst to provide opportunities for the success of my newborn and unborn children. Upon meditating on this one conversation, I realized that I could not be puffed up, because I had the opportunity to obtain my "ultimate goal" in life.

After processing and allowing God to let Uncle Edward's statement resonate in my soul, I concluded that becoming a physician was not at all about me or my ultimate goal, but a much greater gain for God's kingdom. I realized that my medical career would be one of service to others and to be utilized as a stepping stone for my children, grandchildren, and great-grandchildren. God is deliberate in his plans for us as he tells us over and over in his Word; for example, Jeremiah 29:11, (KJV): "For I know the thoughts that I think toward you, saith the LORD, thoughts of peace, and not of evil, to give you an expected end." You see, "it was a setup," as my pastor often says.

God's economic system clearly works. God plants a goal within us. God then sets the stage and cast the characters. God decides who will reap the benefits while uplifting his kingdom as you successfully accomplish his preordained plan for your life.

God's movement toward preparing my life likely started generations before my existence, but for the sake of time I will start with my parents. My father was six years older than my mother, so to assure he met and married the right woman, he was sent off to war, which interrupted his high school years. Upon his release he returned to complete high school and met my mother. Now my mother was born and reared in Richmond,

Texas, but her older sister married and moved to LaGrange and Mother went to live with her sister Tommie Lee. As per God's plan, this placed Mom at LaGrange High School at that perfect time. My mother stated that my father told her the first time they spoke that she was going to be his wife. In less than a year, as was proper to do, he asked her parents' permission to marry her, and there he stayed for sixty-two years until her death. My mother was an exceptionally beautiful woman. She always reminded me that she missed her calling of becoming an actress. However, God placed it on her heart to become a nurse. My mother subsequently exposed me to the medical field, and as a teen I worked in hospitals. I am not sure which came first, me telling my mother I wanted to be a doctor or her telling me I was going to be a doctor. But I do know that numerous things had to fall in place for me to get there, all orchestrated by God.

Let's see how that looks in real life. For years during my childhood, since I was about four years old, I would proudly tell people, "I want to be a pediatrician," knowing well that others would take me seriously for knowing such a big word and such detail. By high school and throughout college, I changed my claim on the future to, "I want to finish college, but my 'ultimate goal' is to become a physician." I stated, imagined, prayed, and wrote my ultimate goal what felt like a million times before I accomplished it. Anyone who knew my parents, my siblings, my cousins, my friends, and especially me, knew "my goal was to become a physician." Some may say I spoke "that thing" into existence. True that. God does tell us in His Word, as a man thinks so is he (Proverbs 23:7a). However, the truth was, not only did God call me to become a physician, he also had a calling for me that pertained to "ultimate goals." We can discuss that in more detail later.

As per Uncle Edward, when we consider the measure of a man, it is not about what he does in his life. Proverbs 13:22a tells us that a good man leaves his children and his children's children an inheritance. We all think of money when we picture this, but with God's economics, money is not the key to wealth. Obedience to God's Word is key. As I was writing this book, my father went on to glory (December 2017). The most precious gift he left was not the home, not the land, not the money in the bank, but rather his legacy of living an upright life before me. This is an inheritance that never stops giving—even through eternity. My parents introducing me to Christ and living godly lives before me has greatly shaped who I am and who my children are today. God's economy is not about the money we make—it is about the life we live, the people we touch, and the service we render to others. My father and mother's home-going celebrations were awesome and standing room only. This was not because of who I am, but the life they lived and their willingness to serve. It was about the people they poured life into over the years. If they did nothing, my siblings and I would do nothing, and my children would do nothing, and the legacy of nothingness will go forth for generations. Only when someone steps in and decides to live their lives according to God's economy will we see the results meant by God, which will be filled with prosperity and wealth. The main lesson here: you will influence a legacy based on what you do, whether positive or negative, good or bad, full of life or destruction.

Consider how often as a child you would say, "I will never say that to my children" or "I would never do that to my children," speaking of your parents' interactions with you. However, as soon as you are grown and dealing with your children, you realize you are doing just what you said you would never do. That is the impact of a legacy. It is hard to avoid it. This is the reason parenting should be intentional and planned, because you will see yourself again, in your children's lives. Legacies are passed on—the good, the bad, and the ugly, if we are not intentional.

PART II

Christ not only orders our steps, but he ordains our circumstances, our goals and our lives. In the Bible in Luke 12:48b (NKJV) we are told: "to whom much is given, from him much will be required". This is a truth which carries over even into parenting.

CHAPTER 4

THE GREAT GAMBLE

"Be honest, are you living a life worth repeating?"

—Dr. KSG

There are several questions you must ask yourself before you decide to begin a family. Am I financially and emotionally fit to be a parent? Many parents do not even stop to consider the commitment and responsibility necessary for rearing children. Next, we must decide, **do we take the time and finances to plan for their lives and future? Do we save for their college education? Do we pray for the child and their future? Lastly, do we include religion in our child's life?**

These are decisions we can control just by making a choice and initiating and implementing a plan.

However, there is another line of questions: Do I prefer a boy or girl? Brown or blue eyes? A nerd or an athlete? Tall or short? These are decisions we do not control. Many would consider this a gamble, but not really. These characteristics are based on genetics and God's plan for that individual.

The real risk is the areas we can influence because God is good for his part. Many decisions we make greatly affect the outcomes of our children. Therefore the parents are the major risk. Whatever you decide, just know that it will influence your child's behavior and decisions as well as their outcomes. If you never mention God, church, or religion, there is a rare chance your child will find God themselves. If they do, they may have encountered pitfalls that may take generations to overcome. Is it our goal to stand by and watch our children wonder through life without any guidance? God forbid.

So the greatest variable in child-rearing is you, the parent. Personally I did not trust myself with the life of my children. My husband and I were asked one question about children during our very brief, one-hour, premarital session by my then beloved pastor, F. W. McIlveen. "Which faith will you rear your children under". At the time we were both Baptists, as was my pastor. My husband was reared Catholic but was baptized into the Baptist denomination about a year or so before we met (God's perfect plan, working in the background). We quite naturally answered, "Baptist." This appeared to be a simple and obvious answer, but when you really think about it, this was an affirmation. A declaration that we would include faith in our children's lives. We made the statement before we even consummated the marriage. God has a way of trying to keep us honest. He will often shape situations and circumstances to guarantee we honor our word. Why? Because God is love, and love is truth. My husband and I first declaring this with a man of God, then God placing the fear of the newborn on my heart, and lastly orchestrating our visit to Indianapolis, IN, and placing me in a conversation with Uncle Edward—all were turns and re-turns that led me to fulfill my declaration to rear my children in God's Word. That is just what he was doing with me. Meanwhile God was preparing my husband as well. Morris was exposed to several ministers, deacons, and older women of God who were pouring into him what God needed to assure he would accept his calling as a minister. Exactly nine years later, while living separately from our family, coaching in Port Arthur, TX, my husband accepted his calling as a preacher. What appeared as random circumstances were all God ordained to assure that we reared our children in a Christ-centered home—in this case, Baptist, as we had spoken to my beloved pastor months before our marriage. Let me stop here and offer another disclaimer. I am not by any means saying becoming a Baptist is the only way. No, sir. In 1 Corinthians chapter 1, Paul reminds us that just as Christ is not divided, neither are we as Christians. Christ started the Church through his disciples. It does not matter who started what denomination. What matters is that we are all of one mind, believers saved by Christ who was crucified for our sins. We subsequently confessed our sins, and our belief led us to baptism in the name of God the Father, God the Son, and God the Holy spirit. Different administrations and different denominations do not matter as long as our faith is based on the one miraculous conception of Christ, His death, and

His resurrection, as imparted to us all through the Word of God. We are the universal Church. The bride of Christ, which He will unite with at his return. So whether Catholic, Methodist, Church of Christ, nondenominational—it really does not matter. One faith, one baptism, one Lord, we are all CHRISTians. One of my favorite deacons growing up often said:

Christian equals CHRIST plus "ian"
Therefore Christian minus Christ equals "ian" = "I am nothing"

So because of God's master plan and provisions, I was convinced based on God's promises that if I reared my children in his Word, the risk was removed, and his Word would direct their paths to make sure they turn and re-turn to Him before their deaths, no matter where life took them.

CHAPTER 5

THE GREAT LOAN

"Legacy, the gift that keeps giving"

—Dr.KSG

Congratulations, your eighteen-year journey has begun. You survived the great gamble. This is where the work begins, right here and right now. You remember the parable of the talents. (Matthew 25). The master gave one man five talents, one man two talents, and the last man one talent before leaving for a trip. While the master was gone the man with five talents invested his, and so did the man with two talents. The man with the one talent allowed fear to overcome him and he decided to bury his talent. When the Master returned he voiced his contentment with the man with five and the man with two talents, respectively, because they both doubled their talents to ten and four. However, he was extremely disappointed with the man with one talent, telling him he could have at least put the talent in a bank so that it could have gained interest.

The lesson here, when God blesses us with something, he expects us to make good with it, and to do all we can to assure the blessings glorify God. This is even true with our children. First, we must realize that we and our children belong to God first and eternally. Our children were loaned to us by God to invest in them and rear them as He has requested, so that we/He can get the best returns.

Loans you may say is a bit drastic. Well, let's quickly look at a life cycle. Many theologians believe we all came from eternity and at a designated time are born into the present for the season we call life. A baby enters this world, and if all goes well he lives with and is reared by his biological or adoptive parents. As infants we must do everything for them—feed them, clean them, clothe them, relate to them, and love them. Scientific studies have shown that infants need eye contact and crave human touch. (JD DM Stack, 2008).[1] This really supports for me the notion that someone was giving them eye contact and touches before they birthed into this world. Jeremiah 1:5a (NASB): "Before I formed you in the womb I knew you." At any rate, the mother's ability to meet the needs of the child does help them develop trust (Erickson's stages- see appendix). This trust last a lifetime unless something tragic happens later in life that destroys the ability to trust. As parents we rear our children and love on them for as long as they allow us. Allow us? Well, think about your relationship with your toddlers. When a parent walks in the door, I can still remember, and oh how I cherished it, the little ones running to me as fast as they could to assure they received my love as they offered the same love with hugs involving their full bodies. What an awesome memory. However,

---

[1] Blackwell Handbook of Infant Development edited by J. Gavin Bremner, Alan Fogel. Chapter 9: Mind knowledge in first year: Understanding attention and intention by Vasudevi Reddy and Chapter 13: The Salience of Touch and Physical Contact during infancy: Unraveling Some of The mysteries of the Somesthetic Sense by Dale M. Stack. Blackwell Publishing 2001

somewhere during "latency" (elementary age), this grand greeting dissipated and changed to a very loud, "Hi, Mom," with or without a hug, dependent on their proximity to the door and what they were engaged in at the time. By teenage years, even if your door makes a bell sound when you arrive home, your teens either yell a hello or only spoke when they happened to pass you or noticed you in the house. Hugs occasionally offered but not necessary daily for the teen. Are you sensing what I am saying here? It's like the loan is almost paid off and the bill collectors no longer call when it is late because you are so close to the payoff.

No matter the case, something happens the older they get. In psychiatry we studied the concept of autonomy, which we see twice in a child's development. As a toddler usually during the "terrible two's" and again as a teen. The definition of autonomy per the *Encarta* dictionary is "a person's independence to make moral decisions and act on them." Yes, two-year-old toddlers believe they know better than you what they should do, just as your teens, when they are going through this life transition. Scientists believe the first presentation of autonomy is for the toddler to transition from being one with the mother to being two individuals. Let me describe this in a way all mothers can relate: Do you remember how many times you have said to your young toddler, "Wait, you are on my feet," when they walk up to you? This is due to your toddler not recognizing you as separate from themselves. In their little world, your feet are their feet, so what is the problem with stepping on them? Not until they go through the transition from oneness with mom to their fight for autonomy will they better respect the boundary between Mom's body and theirs. Now, this is not to say that the three-four year old child, who has completed the transition will not step on your foot out of revenge when you have denied them their favorite toys (smile).

The second time your child goes through autonomy is when they are teens, transitioning to adulthood. Usually there is some rebellion and conflict during this phase, but not always; it is dependent upon the teen's temperament. The conflict is usually a result of the teen recognizing their parents' flaws, which also reveals the teens potential flaws. This can cause resentment to set in. Why is this such a struggle? Well, think about it. In their mind they were born in your image, and if you, as their parents, are not perfect, that may indicate that they will not be perfect, either. At any rate, as stated before, something is changing about this bond.

By age eighteen to twenty-five, the child goes to college, gets a job, and manages to stay away from home and with their peers much more than before. During these years they further detach and begin to develop into adults. Now your communication is more on an as-need basis. They communicate with us when they need or want to, usually not really considering your needs or wants unless you are ill or clearly make your desires known. Parenting our young adults take a very different scale, a very different balance, if I may say so. The prayer is that you have put enough God in them by this time to keep them in the proper places. You know how our money does not grow in checking or savings accounts but may grow better in mutual funds or the like. Yes, it is just like that, only if we have deposited the right stuff can we assure they will remain in the right account. Which is the right account, you ask? The one that is growing and maturing them in Christ.

One thing my husband has always said, "A mother loves her son and rears her daughter and a father loves his daughter and rears his son." This has shown itself as true in my household. I was hard on all my children, but I think my daughter and niece would agree I was harder on them than the boys. I felt more responsible to make sure they developed into strong women of God, but I also had to shape and teach them how to become someone's wife. The thing is, as a woman, I could relate to what they needed to be successful as females. Later in this book I will speak about layaway prayers. They really helped me to shape the development of my young ladies' lives. When my daughter and niece were younger, I knew I had to teach them "humility" and "servitude" while yet not breaking their fight and ambition. I wanted to make sure they knew the difference between love versus manipulation. I also wanted to make sure that their being spoiled was not developing brats. In my home there was a difference between "being spoiled" and "being a brat." Being spoiled meant I get you all of what you need and a whole lot of what you want. The stipulation, you take care of your job: awesome grades and completion of household chores. However, being a brat meant being spoiled and selfish. A brat gets angry if a sibling gets something new and they did not get it, regardless of the need. A brat does not take the time to care or understand others' needs. OK, let me explain this better. For example, I always taught my children that just because the firstborn needs running shoes does not mean everyone gets running shoes. Everyone certainly gets gifts for Christmas, but when it is the second child's birthday, she gets the gift...not everyone. The other thing I intentionally did was give my children money to place in church themselves, from as young as they could walk around the offering table. Likewise, I gave them money at Christmas to buy gifts for each other. One of the greatest lessons, which again only could have come from my God, was taking them to a big Christmas party that the local Child Protective Services (CPS) gave for the children in their custody. I talked to them in advance and asked them to grab a gift from under our Christmas tree with their name on it to take with them to the party for less fortunate children. The first year they went, my baby boy Rion was relatively young, maybe three or four. He was good until we arrived and he saw how many gifts were under the humongous Christmas tree. I remember him crying and saying he wanted to keep his gift. I tried to explain, "No, we are going to give to the children in need." And he said to me, "I am the needy." At any rate, by the end of the night when he saw that all of those children received one gift and were ecstatic and he knew he had at least three more at home under the tree with his name, he understood what "needy" meant. From that day on, this same child would come home from school and ask if he could offer a pair of his athletic shoes to a classmate who needed shoes. Train up a child and you better know that my God will do it every time! Praise break…

Back to the concept of our children as loans. Subsequently our young adults graduate from college, start careers, and move into their own places, only to marry, have children, and begin the process over. We therefore have a limited amount of time to invest in our children all that we can to assure they will be returned better than they started. It is almost as if my God loans us a shell (the child's physical body) and the inner shell with a seed of God's spirit and says, "Take this shell and fill it with all that I need it to have to become the person I purposed them to be." It is our decision as parents to participate. Will we assist God to build the shell from the inside out using all that God has given us? Or will we do nothing and allow the world to destroy the spirit by filling the shell with worldly dark spirits, which operate in place of the sweet Holy Spirit? The latter is a "dead" being, and what parent in their right mind want a living "dead" child?

The lesson here is just like the parable we spoke of at the beginning of this chapter. God expects the talents (our children) he loans to us to multiply. This meant that the recipients of the talents in the Bible had to think, strategize, and use their resources to assure they multiplied the talents. The same is true in parenting. We as parents must think, plan, pray, strategize, and use our resources (the Bible, Sunday school, life lessons, education, our parents' examples, prayers, and the guidance of the Holy Spirit) to assure we gain the *returns* God expects.

PART III

God trust us as parents, the stakes are high, but the rewards are great. Go in for the win and don't forget to take the Word with you throughout the journey.

CHAPTER 6

KNOW YOUR ASSETS AND LIABILITIES AS A PARENT

"Life lessons sometimes come in small packages."

—Dr. KSG

As a young mother with limited experience with little babies, I had to recognize my liabilities. I always loved babies and wanted to hold them whenever visiting anyone with an infant, but my knowledge and understanding of them was zip/nada/absentee. As a medical student I studied developmental milestones during my clinical rotation in pediatrics. I also knew the signs and symptoms of an ill infant, but as for a healthy baby who depended on me 24/7, I was in for a great awakening. This, my dear, was an intimidating liability for me.

The element of surprise came as early as the pregnancy. I do not remember how healthy or unhealthy my diet was at this time, now thirty years ago, but two things I ate quite often: mustard greens from my Aunt Bessie's garden and watermelons. My first child was born with two birthmarks, one looked like a leaf of a mustard green and the other a red mark that looked like a plump watermelon. Here is the issue. Watermelon is full of sugar and water, and boy was I full of fluid. I had about thirty pounds of water shed from my body after that boy was born. At any rate, I had no idea how much weight I could and would gain from eating watermelon daily. My husband so kindly delivered two per week to our home. A whole watermelon became a part of our kitchen décor. I literally ate one-fourth of a watermelon for my midmorning snack and the same for my late-night snack. Sounds healthy, right? No. Watermelon is healthy in moderation. It is composed of water, electrolytes, antioxidants, and other natural and healthy ingredients. But like all fruit it also has sugar. You know, too much of anything is not good. At any rate, I gained almost fifty pounds with my firstborn, which was not very healthy at all. So I share this to say educate yourself well before even conceiving so that you will not put undue stress on your body during your child-bearing years. I so admire those who can have babies and return to their former weight, not so with me. From watching others there are a few things I anecdotally believe can help in this area:

1) The amount of physical activity you partake in during your adult years prior to considering pregnancy can be beneficial. I was involved in competitive sports in high school, but I gave that up in college. I periodically played with softball leagues, played basketball or volleyball, but rarely worked out. Personally I do believe that the young ladies who carry on with competitive athletics through college somehow prolong the accelerated metabolism. (By the way, an explanation of anecdotal: only a theory or hypothesis, usually based on personal observations—no research to support this opinion.)

2) Those who seek personal trainers' assistance soon after their childbirth appear to return to their previous weight.

3) Plain and simple good genes. This is interesting and can be deceptive because good genes to remain slim do not always mean you are maintaining your health. (Dr. KSG tip: Don't let your weight be mistaken for your health.)

At any rate, I did not meet either of these three conditions. Therefore after each of my three pregnancies, I added to my body mass, and today I continue to watch and monitor, fighting to keep the scale from moving in the same direction as my age. OK, back to the subject at hand. Know your assets and your liabilities. I define intelligence as not only what you know but, also your ability to acquire what you need by utilizing your resources wisely. I quickly learned that the Dr. Spock book and other such parenting books were not for me and my household. Therefore to get what I needed, I had to use the number one selling book, the "Holy Bible." I also appreciated wise counsel from select women whose babies survived their first year of life and appeared to be thriving, such as my good friend who wrote the foreword in this book.

Simply spoken, what you know and have available to you are your assets in this chapter. What you don't know and must seek elsewhere is yet another burden. Since you know what you know, there is no need to visit that. Let's focus on what you don't know.

As a young mother, I had no idea how to get my baby to stay asleep all night. Some may even argue that it is not healthy for a young infant (less than four weeks) to sleep throughout the night. When your baby is awakening every two hours and ready to play hopscotch at 2 a.m., you will agree, if I can get him to sleep, please let him sleep. As a working mother and one who needs six hours of sleep to function, my goal, to survive, was to get him sleeping at least six hours per night. So I sought wisdom, and my mother-in-law who reared six children and previously owned a twenty-four-hour day care, shared a pearl of wisdom that worked for all three of my children and saved my life. The key here my dear mothers, is attention to details and patience.

If it worked three times for me, I have faith that if you do it right, it will work for you. First, let's clarify what we mean by sleeping all night. For a young infant (four to twelve weeks), sleeping all night is equal to five to six hours. I know that ten to twelve hours is desired especially by a sleep-deprived mother, but that would cause your baby to miss too many meals, so let's strive for five to six hours per night. Just thought I may need to clarify. OK, here it is, and I have structured the method into four simple steps.

a. Work hard to keep your baby awake between the hours of 7 p.m. to 10 p.m. at night. This can be a struggle, but I promise your baby will eventually sleep more hours as you train them to adapt to your schedule.

b. At 9 p.m. give your baby that nice warm bath that always sets the tone for a good night's sleep. I always loved to lotion down my baby after drying him. It is like a baby massage while still getting him ready for that good night of sleep. (Dr. KSG safety tip for siblings: I always taught my toddlers to only kiss and touch the feet and legs of our baby to avoid injuries to the eyes or face and extra emergency room visits. If they are awake when I lotion the baby, I allow them to lotion the legs and feet. This invites your toddler to love on the baby rather than viewing him as one big "no-no," leaving big brother or sister feeling angry, isolated, and unattached.)

c. Feed the baby as per pediatrician guidelines. My firstborn grew fast—the new guideline is based on age. When cereal is allowed, use it in the last meal of the night. Just because it is cereal does not mean it is just for breakfast. Cereal is to babies as steak and potatoes are to daddies. Don't miss this step at bedtime. A good feeding and a dry diaper are essential before bedtime. Put the baby to sleep and you go to sleep also, in separate beds, please.

d. Now the specifics per Grandma Curry: any mother can relate to this descriptor, but first-time expecting moms will have to figure this part out. You see, babies typically take about thirty minutes to really, really wake up. Often young mothers hear them squirming. New mommies know this is what most of us say: "OK, the baby is waking up. Let me enjoy this last thirty minutes of sleep." Here lies our mistake. Don't wait for the thirty-minute full-blown outcry, no, don't go for this sucker punch. Instead get up as soon as the squirming starts. Learn to change the baby's diaper without even picking him up or moving anything other than his bottom. The first night or two, you may pick him up and feed him. If you get up right away, their eyes will be closed, and the baby never fully wakes up. They will eat, burp, and allow you to change their diaper and remain in the slumbering mode the entire time.

You repeat this every night, eventually it will get to the point where the baby does not have to eat. Only the diaper will need to be changed. Finally, your little infant will eventually sleep all the way through until about 5 a.m., without even needing the diaper changed.

I promise this will work. My first baby was sleeping all night in two weeks, my second in four, and my last in six weeks. Don't ask me the reason for such diversity. My guess is temperament and birth weight. The process took a little bit of grit, but it was manageable. The babies were not waking up three and four times a night once I started the process; at the most, once. I trust this process. It worked three times for me and I have shared it with a few others who have had success. Godspeed to all new mothers. Five to six hours of uninterrupted sleep for a new mother is such a blessing.

CHAPTER 7

GOD'S GIFT

"Behold, children are a gift of the LORD, The fruit of the womb is a reward." (NASB)

—PSALM 127:3

A cool November evening, Tuesday, 7:29 PM. "It's a banana head boy," my doctor yelled out after we were all holding our breaths when I had to push one last time, after his head cleared. Yes, after his head cleared. The doctor murmured, "Oh my, is it two babies here?" The answer was no, but the broad shoulders of my baby boy required an extra push because his head kindly conformed to flow with the passage, but his broad shoulders would not give. Despite all my degrees, rewards, and accomplishments, that moment was by far the most satisfying of my life. I no longer had to carry the extra fifty pounds I gained with this baby. My husband yelled, "Yes, it's a boy. Now you don't have to have ten." I felt accomplished that the tantrum I threw in the doctor's office worked. There was not an eleventh-day delay; ten days were beyond what was humanly possible in my eyes. Oh, and Thanksgiving. He was born two days before Thanksgiving, so I would be on time for Thanksgiving dinner, so I thought. Not that I was cooking, but my cousin Linda, who is the best cook ever, would be hosting the dinner. Yes, accomplished was the feeling of the moment, until they laid that long baby boy in my arms. Instantly fear hit me. *What do I do with this? Will he survive my inexperience?* Prayers rushed through my mind, thanking God for ten toes and ten fingers, as my college roommate, Lavon, mother of six, always told me to do first, but also asking God if I was equipped to take care of this darling little person.

Yes, these little people come into our world and it is never the same. I have learned that what I invest and pour into my children is directly proportionate to what I get out. God's economy: "You reap what you sow," even in child-rearing. I think I first learned this from my mother. I must warn you up front, this is where I really got things twisted, and some fifty years later actually, as I wrote this book, I finally received truth. I want to say the following is a life-transforming moment. Allow me to explain.

Before my mother had me, she had all boys. She told me she prayed Hannah's Prayer. I will summarize from 1 Samuel 1:10–11: Hannah promised God if he gave her a son she would give him back to God and that scissors would never touch his hair. So likewise my mother, desperately wanting a girl, prayed and told God if He gave her a girl (me), she would give me back to Him. Hearing this all my life was sometimes scary. As soon as I learned to read, I wanted to know more about this child promised back to God. As it turned out Samson was not the only child to whom the Nazarene vow was bestowed. (*NAZIRITE*: a person who vows for a specific period to abstain from partaking of grapes or any of its products, whether intoxicating or not, cutting his hair, and touching a corpse Number 6:3–9). Hannah was the prophet Samuel's mother, but when my mother mentioned that her son's hair would never be cut, my young mind-set instantly went to the infamous Samson. Therefore I related my birth and destiny for many years to the life of Samson. The following is my memory of the experience using the erroneous information: Samuel the prophet not Samson was the son of Hannah, but as a child and for many of my adult years, I never noticed my error as I related my life to Samson.

Hannah gave Samson (Samuel) to the religious leaders to rear when he was old enough to wean; most scholars estimate three to six years old. I knew this would not happen due to the fact that my dad would have lost his mind had my mother taken me away from him, so I felt I was safe there. I watched my mother's rendition of keeping her promise to give me back to God by making sure to have me in Sunday school, children's church, choir rehearsal, and worship services routinely. "Routinely." Let me clarify: every time the church doors opened, we were there. I was a believer and baptized by the age of three years old. Just recently my older brother, Floyd asked if I remembered singing hymns like a grown woman when I was three years old. I must admit, I did not, but it fit with my theory of how my mother kept her promise to give me back to God. She exposed me to prayer meetings, missionary work, and serving others. My life, as a result, was not easy and certainly not sin free, but the Holy Spirit always convicted me and made a way to bring me to right standing with God, urging me to repent. This allowed my mother to see me reach my ultimate goal of becoming a medical doctor, as well as to see and hear me teach spiritual and godly lessons to youth and women in many venues. Likewise, I watched her do the same. Her greatest ministry, in my opinion, was praying and making disciples for God's kingdom. She definitely passed down this legacy and I cheerfully accepted. My point here is if giving me back to God, as my mother promised, played a role in bringing me closer to God, I decided I would indeed give my son back to God, and not just him but all of my children.

I remind you this is God's economy. Remember, Matthew 18:18 tells us whatever we loose on earth will be loosed in heaven and whatever we bind on earth will be bound in Heaven. God's economy says that whatever you are willing to release over to Him, He will bring back to you, pressed down and flowing over with blessings (Luke 6:38). He is faithful like that. The more we seek Him, the more of Him we find. The more we speak to Him, the more clearly we hear Him speak. The more we give, the more He gives back to us. God has a perfect economy system and it can be used with rearing our children. The more we expose and give our children to His kingdom, the more He uses them and gives toward their earthly possessions. If we pour lots of godly things into our children, they will deliver godly things back to the universe. This is the reason I never understood parents who curse their children. Pouring in negativity can bring back negativity. I thought if I poured in God's Word, I will have a greater chance to get back behaviors, attitudes, and accomplishments that look like God's Word. I can remember often telling christian parents who brought their children to see me for psychiatric counsel, "I prescribe Sunday school." I remember once reading about a local judge whose sentence for a delinquent teen was "Sunday school." Pouring in the Word of God, not just at home but also in an established Bible-teaching church, can convict your child and replace unwanted behaviors with more godly behaviors. His Word does not return void.

It was settled, before we even left the hospital, because I was so fearful of messing up my little man, I decided when they laid him in my arms, less than ten minutes old, I would give him back to God by pouring scripture into him to increase my chance of a purposeful return.

CHAPTER 8

THE GREAT INVESTMENT

"For by your standard of measure it will be measured to you in return."(NASB)

—LUKE 6:38B

I t is this portion of that scripture that rang in my soul. This one statement is the epitome of God's economy.

- It likens to: "Do unto others." How you treat others, you will be treated.
- It likens to: "An eye for an eye." What you do to others will be done back to you.
- It likens to: "What you loose on earth will be loosed in heaven." We ignore Him on earth, He ignores us in heaven.

- It likens to: "Forgive others as you would like to be forgiven." You can't forgive, you can't be forgiven.

We must really take heed and pay attention to how we treat others and how we treat God. Our behaviors, whether positive or negative, will have natural consequences. What we give will be given back to us in the same manner, if not more so. If given with a grudge, then things will come back to us grudgingly. If we give generously, things will come back to us generously.

You may ask, how does this relate to rearing children? Let me explain. What we put into parenting will manifest what comes out. My logic said to me, three children under five and more children than adults in a home could mean trouble. I wanted to even the playing field. Some would hire a nanny. I chose a teenager from my local church who spent quite a bit of time with us until she went off to college. She spent school nights and summers with us and traveled on vacations with us. I even helped her secure a part-time job at their elementary school to satisfy her vocational coop class requirements, during her senior year of high school. Yes, she was a blessing. She was a great helper and she became a great friend of my family. I was a working mother, a physician with a private practice and a professor at the local medical school. My husband was a high school football/track coach and later a high school administrator. Our hours away from home were vast. In addition to this my husband was a minister by the time my children's ages ranged from three to nine years old. I say all of this to help paint the picture for how important it was for me to make some healthy investments into my children before they formed their own little opinions about life, basically from five to seven.[2] Personally, I believe, if you have not begun to tap into the spirituality of your child by age six, you may have to undo some of their thinking as you teach them God's Word. Biblically, mothers who were giving their sons for the priesthood would

---

[2] Angela Oswalt, MSW, "Childhood Cognitive Development: Information Processing," accessed February 5, 2019, https://www.mentalhelp.net/ARTICLES/EARLY-CHILDHOOD-COGNITIVE-DEVELOPMENT-INFORMATION-PROCESSING/

do it soon after they weaned from breastfeeding, which appears to be at approximately age three.[3]

My investments came in various shapes and forms. First I invested my **prayers**. In addition I wanted to make sure my children understood the rewards of a healthy prayer life. One of the most important things I did daily with them, we will discuss later. However, to maximize intimate moments, I promised myself that I would bathe my children myself when they were young toddlers and I would tuck them in every night. Now tuck in was a routine that I am sure they could tell you in unison. Of course they may remember it differently from their fifty-eight-year-old mother, but this is my version.

Two hours before my desired bedtime I would start my routine. I remember that because their ages were two to six years apart and they had at least thirty-minute windows between their bedtimes. I started with the baby boy. Luckily he was a wise old soul in a little boy's body. He rarely

---

[3] John F. Walvoord and Roy B. Zuck. *The Bible Knowledge Commentary (Old Testament) Book 1*, (Colorado Springs: Cook Communication Ministries, 1983 and 2004), 434.

stayed up past 7:30 p.m. I typically would have him bathed and in bed by 7:00 p.m. The routine: read a book, say prayers, and then I would sing the "Lord's Prayer" to him. Thirty minutes later I would read a book to the oldest two and one at a time tuck in with individual prayers and then singing the "Lord's Prayer." Every night, three times or more, if someone had difficulty falling asleep, I would sing the "Lord's Prayer." They did not know this, but often after they fell asleep I would walk the hallway, stopping by each room to do what I called "putting prayers in the layaway." That is, prayers for their next day, next challenge, their futures, including their purity and the purity of their future spouses. This made it so easy for me to reassure my daughter-in-love that I prayed for her all her life, because it was true. Many prayers were laid up in heaven to make sure that my young men found their God-ordained ribs (wives) and that my daughter would be found by the man God has for her. God confirmed that he heard my "layaway prayers" with my oldest son's wife. First, in the center of my right hand the lines look like an "M" and "K" connected. Important only because my husband's first initial is "M" and mine is "K."

Purposely I named my daughter Cassie, but with a "K," "Kassie." God's perfect little winks confirmed that I prayed for the right daughter-in-love. Her parents had the same first initials as my husband and I. "M and K," even more specifically her mother and I share the same first name, Kathy. Lastly, her mother purposely named my daughter-in-love Crystal with a "K," "Krystal." Did I mention that both of our husbands' initials were MG and that their family were born-again Christians who lived a life of integrity? This may all sound like a coincidence to you, but God and I have a history of Him revealing His love for me in signs. This, my friend, was just another clear sign from God that my "layaway prayers" were heard and being answered. Excuse me for a praise break...

OK, where was I? Oh yes, those "layaway prayers." Let me say a little more about this. So many adults today will tell you they lived off the prayers of their grandparents or parents until they came to know God personally for themselves. This is another reason why layaway prayers are so important. I did not know the path God had for my children's lives. I did not know what ages they would accept Christ as their personal Savior, but

I knew it would happen. I wanted enough prayers stored up to assure the prayers could take them to their point of spiritual independence. More importantly, even for ourselves we need prayers in the layaway for rainy days. God tells us to pray without ceasing (1 Thessalonians 5:17). This means to pray always so that if a storm that obscures your spiritual vision comes, you are still covered by the many prayers you have stored in the layaway.

Now back to the "tuck in" phase, this is just one example of my investment in the spiritual well-being of my children. This was a great time and done throughout their elementary years. This investment was a joy for me. Remember, I told you how afraid I was of becoming a parent. It was not because I did not have great parents as examples, but I was the baby of my family. Therefore by the time my parents had me they were "professional parents," it seemed. They appeared older and wiser in my eyes. Here I was a young lady in my early thirties with three babies whom I had no clue how to shape. I did, however, believe God's Word.

Psalm 37:25 (NASB): "I have been young and now I am old, Yet I have not seen the righteous forsaken or his descendants begging bread."

This scripture said to me: "Kathy, you really don't want your children to ever starve or beg for food, so to cover them and make sure this never happens, you must invest in some **righteousness**." I needed to be as much like Christ as possible to offer this guaranteed return to my children. This is indeed what I did. My mantra and go-to song of praise became: "Lord, I want to be a Christian in my heart. Moreover, Lord, I want to be like Jesus in my heart." I stayed in the church and stayed in the Word of God. This was an easy investment for me because of my upbringing. This just meant to keep doing what I grew up doing and what I watched my parents do throughout the years. You know the routine, Sunday school, two to three services per Sunday, and of course good ole Baptist Training Union (BTU). During the week, prayer meeting/ Bible study/choir rehearsal, and youth church. Please do not forget, Vacation Bible School in the summers, and not just your church but every church within walking distance in the neighborhood. Some of you know the routine; we entered, every time the church doors opened. I reasoned, *Drill this routine into them and they may not make all of the services as adults, but they will at least make some.* Likewise, they will never be beggars or so poor that they cannot eat due to their mother and father living righteously and our God keeping His promise. This is another example of turning toward God and He will guide your path. This is just what He did. He led my husband and I as we led our children. I must stop here to interject a warning sign or two. Let's call them "red flags." Can you see the potential error here? Red flag # 1: the big "L" word. You know, legalism. You are familiar, right? As per the dictionary: strict adherence to a literal interpretation of a law, rule, or religious moral code. Yes, I was really living a legalistic life when my children were young. You know the Bible tells us when our path is crooked, God will straighten it for us. He did just that. He led my husband and I to attend a local biblical college to obtain a bachelor's degree in biblical leadership. It was here that God helped me to recognize how legalistic I had become. I religiously attended church, all services, all meetings, dressed a certain way and behaved a certain way, not just at church but home as well. Worse than that, I expected and sometimes harassed others to do the same. I feel I was older in my thirties than I am in my near sixties. Legalism is a waste of energy, time, and resources. We are unable to be perfect with rules and regulations. This is the reason why God has us under grace rather than the Law. Legalism has run so many young people away from the Church. Think about it, when we are practicing legalism we have disobeyed the greatest of all commandments: to love the Lord our God with all our hearts. If I am focusing on obeying rules and laws, I am not getting to know God and His love toward me. We should not read and study God's Word to master the laws, but rather to get to know him more intimately. Legalism is a great sin and it can kill your evangelistic efforts, even with your own children.

Red flag #2: hypocritical lifestyles. That is, those who behave one way at home and a totally different way in the church. This reminds me of a discussion we had with our oldest son about "preacher's kids." This is a term coined to describe the preacher's child, specifically ridiculing those whose behavior is subpar. "The preacher's kids" behavior and attitude are scrutinized when deemed unacceptable and worldly. My husband was warning our son to be watchful and not fall into the trap of a "rebellious preacher's kid." My son kindly reminded us that because we were living a life of integrity, he had no confusion about God's expectations. My son believed that "rebellious preacher's kids" are developed by observing their parents live a double life right before their eyes. Children see their parents' actions and they do take notes. We are called to a standard of integrity, which is doing the right thing, even when people are not watching. Yes, it is true that sometimes our children must face obstacles and setbacks to become who God called them to be, which becomes their testimony. However, we as parents should make sure that we are living a life of integrity before our children, because just as God is watching, so are our little ones. Our children are more likely to do what they see us do. You can show them much better than you can tell them. Children are very good at imitating and playing the recorder of life right back to our faces.

I say all this to say not only did I invest my prayers and righteousness in my children, I invested in my **morals** and **values**. I know God straightened my crooked paths in parenthood, but in retrospect I thought the years of legalistic living was a big mistake and a waste. I have since realized, or rather God revealed to me, that children are very concrete. They see everything as black or white. No gray zones and no in between. I do believe that it helped my children to see us strictly live the lives we preached and taught. This at least set a pattern for them to apply some wisdom in their daily choices as they became adults. My husband and I were both no longer drinkers when we married (both for different reasons), neither of us smoked, and we did not use foul language. My children to this day insist that I did curse them at least once when they were young. I usually refute this, but in hindsight, if it was only once, I have to say, "Look at God." Strangely enough, realizing the enemy is always on his job, after more than twenty years without cursing, I do remember using a curse word with my daughter while writing this book. She tried to keep me from using her phone, which at the time I paid for the monthly bill. "Girl, give me that damn phone." OK, so twice in their lives. I repented right away and apologized to her as well, on the spot. But I still scream, "LOOK AT GOD!" I was never one who used a lot of profanity in my younger days, but if the wrong button was pushed you know what followed. HELP ME SAY DELIVERANCE! Praise break...

Investing in child-rearing really speaks to what we place into our children. Let me share this story to clarify. I remember when my oldest was approaching two, let's say about fourteen months. I decided to conduct an experiment in child-rearing. Everyone refers to children at this age as "the terrible twos." Even in my studies as a child psychiatrist we were trained that "no" was the favorite word of the two-year-old child. So I decided, in my naivety, that I would make my child a pilot study (a test baby). I would not have a "no-saying terrible two toddler." To assure this, my husband and I never said no to our eldest son from fifteen to thirty-six months of age. Truth is, the word "no" is not what makes a two-year-old terrible. It is not what they say; it is the attitude and persistent desire to be their own boss (autonomy) that drives their behavior. So true enough, my eldest son never used the word "no," but he had no problem getting his point across when his desire was contrary to ours.

The positive to this is that I learned to offer options and Braylon learned to choose from the options offered. I did not share this story because it had an outstandingly positive outcome, but rather to share a different lesson. This pilot study, orchestrated and designed by yours truly, added no positive dividends to my child's life. It was my design and my doing based on my knowledge in child development, as a then child and adolescent psychiatry fellow in training. I am not arguing against psychological interventions, but they are not fail-proof and do not give the automatic and persistent results of God's Word. If anything, this self-developed research project backfired. Personally I feel my eldest became uncomfortable with the word no. He never threw tantrums or anything like that, beyond two years of age, but throughout his life it appeared that "no" was senseless to him, a lack of creativity or inability to reason and offer options. No was not a word he seemed to embrace. He was super compliant and rarely disobeyed, but he wrestled with the purpose for the negativity, of the word "no." I think he just never quite understood why anyone would say no to him, especially since he worked so hard to be the best student, best athlete, best person, and best Christian he could be. This is the child who in seventh grade needed to confirm that fouling in basketball was not a sin. I credit the pilot for just confusing my child about the use of the word "no." He missed learning that sometimes people say no just because they can, without explanation, rhyme, or reason. Even more importantly, he later had to learn that sometimes God says no because He knows all and can see all. Braylon had to learn early in his adult life that "no" is not always a direct attack against him, but sometimes protection for him.

I say all of this to ask you to be careful about thinking and believing that you must do things as the "secular" scholars say that you should. We as Christians have access to the Scholar of all scholars, the absolute best-selling Author of all best-selling authors. The one and only Word of God, which has been on the best-selling list for thousands of years without requiring any upgraded editions. Don't make my mistake of exploring with your own intellect when you can line up with His divine and ordained way, which will bring you the greatest return on your investment, every time, without fail. Enough on the red flags and back to the investments as parents.

Another great investment is **time**. Yes, good old quality time. I realized in retrospect that the reason time with our children is so important has to do with spiritual development, physical development, and unity as a family. Physically, scientist have done studies with very young infants showing "failure to thrive" if they have minimal to no interaction with other humans.[4]

Time with anyone nurtures the relationship and the same is true with our children. Our children will take the values and experiences offered them to the next generation. When your children are young, eight or less, begin a routine of allowing them time to talk to you, times for devoted listening to them. A great time individually was during their personal tuck-in time; they knew that they could use that time to share whatever they wanted about their day. Rides to or from school were also utilized either for Bible reading or talking. I

---

[4] Kenneth S. Robson, "The Role of Eye-to-Eye Contact in Maternal-Infant Attachment," accessed February 5, 2019, https://onlinelibrary.wiley.com/doi/abs/10.1111/j.1469-7610.1967.tb02176.x.

took seriously the instructions in Deuteronomy 6, which basically tells us to always teach our children God's Word, in our going and coming, at our tables, and so forth. Bottom line: use every opportunity you can to teach God's precepts.

In addition to talking, ensure you allow your child **time to play** and be happy in your presence, and time to cry in your presence. Learn as a parent to tolerate emotions; you are the best teacher for your child regarding learning to control their emotions (fear, sadness, anger, or excitement). If you always send them away as children when crying, when they become emotional teens, they will automatically turn away from you because this is what you have modeled. My husband and I always kept an open-door policy for our children to come to us with any issue or problem. Just as we need time to get to know our future spouses, time to know our one and only God, we also need time to know our children. This reminds me of a story from my baby boy's kindergarten year. First, he always told me that his teacher was not teaching the phonics for the vowels correctly. He learned them as a pre-K very well. I knew my child and knew he was likely right, but not until the end of the school year when a class action suit was filed by a group of parents against the school was this confirmed. At any rate, one day his teacher met me at the door and stated that Rion threw a rock and hit a little girl during recess. I asked her if it was an accident and she stated no, that he did it on purpose. Knowing my child, I knew better. I said, "Did you ask him?" And she stated, "Yes, he said he did it on purpose." I suggested that the two us should go talk to him. Mind you I am a child psychiatrist and I speak to little children all day about their negative behaviors. The dialogue proceeded as follows:

Me: "Rion, what happened today at recess?"
Rion: "I hit Sarah with a rock."
Me: "Was it an accident?"
Rion: "No, I meant to throw the rock."
Me: "Why?"
Rion: "Shawn and I were playing a game to see who could throw the farthest."
Me: "Did you mean for the rock to hit Sarah?"
Rion: "No, that was an accident."
Me: "Did you apologize?
Rion: "Yes, I ran to her and said I was sorry, and I told the teacher she was hurt."

I turned to the teacher and stated, "See, you asked the wrong question. He did throw the rock on purpose, but did he want it to hit Sarah? No." I share this because I regularly talked to my child and knew how he utilized words. That day I changed the trajectory of a teacher's view, which could have changed my son's positive experience of school. Can you imagine the negative places this experience could have gone? Negative write up in my son's folder, a shouting match with the teacher, or my son getting blamed for something malicious that was innocent. (Dr. KSG tip: talk to your children regularly about their little experiences, so that when something major arises, you can advocate for them with confidence.) Parents, remember, if you blow them off as children, they will certainly blow you off as teens and young adults.

Lastly, as parents we need to take the **time to read and study the Bible with our children**. Not just what they receive from church but also in the home. I reared my children on Proverbs from very early ages, like four to eleven years of age; we read Proverbs daily together. This was done in the car rides to school in the mornings. We would read and discuss at least one to two verses a day. I found it to be easy reading for explaining God's statutes to my children. In addition we would periodically have Bible studies in our family room, just spontaneously from other books of the Bible. And once they were older, like middle and high school years, we had a few days a week that my husband planned early morning family Bible study and prayer time at the kitchen table. We know the Bible tells us "Faith comes by hearing" Romans 10:17 (NKJV). Some people believe that is from hearing the preacher's sermon only, but faith also comes by hearing yourself read God's Word. The Word can be contagious, so I wanted to expose my children to enough early on so that it would be a refuge for them in times of trouble. In addition it is my prayer that they desire to read the Bible more and more on their own, knowing that this would increase their faith. This may seem like a bit much, but it really was not. I had forgotten all about the early morning Bible studies until one morning, when my husband and I were praying with Rion, as he left to do a presentation for work, he reminded us. As parents we have eighteen years to pour the love of God into our children, and let me tell you that time flies by very quickly.

Part IV

This section can be referred to as risky business. It covers our awareness of setbacks and pitfalls. This is the time when we separate the "men from the boys" and the "rocks from the pebbles."

CHAPTER 9

THE GREAT DEPRESSION

"Love with forgiveness heals all brokenness."
—Dr. KSG

As I stated before, bedtime rituals were a great part of my children's lives from the age of the first turning one until the last one turned twelve. Nightly I went upstairs, read, said a prayer, and then sang the "Lord's Prayer." During their teenage years, I encouraged them to read the Bible before saying their prayers and going to sleep. Even as teens, I often went up and offered each of them the time to speak with me individually before falling asleep. I will never forget the night in 2006, when my son came to me as I sat relaxing in a recliner after dinner was served, the kitchen cleaned, and his siblings had already turned in for the night. He typically would have been upstairs doing home-work. Advance placement (AP) classes were a must in my home, but he instead came very close to my side and looked at me with the most disap-pointed look known to man and said, "Mom, I'm in trouble." My heart dropped to the floor. This child had never given me an ounce of trouble. He was a junior in high school making straight A's in all AP classes, star football/basketball/track athlete, and the absolute best example of a big brother you could ask for, and nearly in tears he was now tell-ing me, "Mom, I am in trouble." I sat up instantly, turned down the TV's volume, thinking simul-taneously, how did my husband get to miss this? Thoughts rushed through my mind in that milli-second as he exhaled. I thought, *I'm not ready to be a grandmother.* Pause right there, because instantly my mind went to that place, the Great Depression, the great downfall, the great setback that would affect my child's life forever.

Often while rearing children, the day comes when your child does something that appears to be the onset of destruction. The road that can never bring them back. This may include teen pregnancy or parenting, dropping out of school/ college, delinquent behaviors, or substance-use disorder. Those were the worries of the 90s. Now victimization, violence, pornography, racial profiling, gender identity, and substance-use disorder are more common, but all can open the door for the Great Depression. Whatever the case as parents we often began to project ahead to where this catastrophe can take them. It can clearly feel like the end of the world.

However, as parents, after the initial shock, we must regain focus to show that we have gained interest on our investment when the Master returns. This maybe an excellent opportunity to self-reflect. Look at our life as parents. Where am I falling short? To this day, right or wrong, if my children suffer, I quickly ask myself if I am praying enough. This is my internal battle daily; maybe even my thorn in the side. When I die my children are going to find so many prayer journals. I have written enough prayers to have a collection called the encyclopedia of prayers. At any rate, when these great depressions hit, self-reflect to assure you both grow spiritually. You remain supportive and you offer supplication—that is, desperately interceding in prayer for your child. The goal is always to survive and return from the Great Depression. No experience, no matter how negative, dictates the type of life or future your child will have. Your remaining supportive, prayerful, and positive can be the catalyst for a revelation and change for the better. I, for example, watched my mother pray for her son Robert to be healed from his addiction for what seemed like twenty years. When he was delivered, now twenty-plus years sober, they both gave God the glory and he now serves as a deacon at his church.

Our success as parents is measured by the success of our children. Therefore when the moment comes that your child says, "Mom, I'm in trouble," do like our heavenly Father did for us: He found a solution and He prayed that we would accept it.

"Mom, I'm in trouble." Oh, I'm sure you want to hear the rest of the story. With the straightest nonjudgmental and welcoming expression I could muster up, I said, "What's wrong, son?" He went on to tell me he made an "F" on a major project for his AP History class. *Hallelujah!* I shouted internally. Now this was disappointing, more so for him than me, but I did remain in character, asking, "What happened?" He went on to explain that a team-mate insisted on being his partner for the project but planned to have my son do all the work. The friend's mother later apologized. She knew how difficult it must have been for my son to get the "F" but was glad he stood for what was right. My son sacrificed his grade to avoid being manipulated. I don't remember how this all played out, but I do know his grade did not fall below a B on his report card, because that I would remember.

This example of course is not as serious as some we have all heard or experienced. It does, however, remind us as parents that our children will have ups and downs and they may fall, but just like the economy rebounds from the great depression, if we all continue to pray, deposit, and invest, our children will likewise rebound.

CHAPTER 10

BANKRUPTCY HITS HOME

"Emptiness drains possibilities."

—Dr. KSG

The adjective bankrupt as declared by law describes one unable to pay outstanding debts. Bankrupt as a noun is a person judged by a court to be in more debt than they have funds to pay. The bankrupt's property can be taken and disposed of for the benefit of creditors.

Stretching the imagination, a bankrupt parent is unable to meet the commitment that comes with parenting a child. We naturally think of the "deadbeat parent." OK, let's be real, the "deadbeat dad." However, this chapter is not to speak to that at all. Rather to the bankruptcy of confidence that hits the parents and the children when they learn that the family unit as they know it is dissolving or disappearing. We can physically see the missing spouse as disposed-of property, completely disengaged and dissolved. In fact, some couples rush to court because they believe this helps them to heal and move on to their own personal agendas. However, we cannot physically see the bankrupt souls of the parents and children left empty handed. The vast emptiness affects every adult and child in the home. Family portraits become useless, as if the memories could be dissolved along with the marriage. I want to address this catastrophe from three very different angles, which I believe are crucial to discuss when addressing parenting. The main thing I want to impress here is that the "missing parent" has just as much influence over your child's development as the present parent.

Bankruptcy by Divorce

First let's tackle divorce. I can say without hesitation that I hate divorce. I don't hate the people, but I hate "divorce." I have watched it drain the life out of so many people I love dearly. I could stay on that subject alone, but that is for a different book. Let's stay focused on the task at hand.

When we hear divorce within a family we instantly focus on the husband and wife and often underestimate the emotional bankruptcy it causes in the children. I am not here to bash those who have faced this tragedy; nobody wants to go through this season. Divorce is not easy for anyone, no matter the circumstances or reasons. Very often we see the divorcees after the struggle and assume it was all peaches and cream, but I assure you, if they are transparent, this was not a fun day in the park for any couple. Therefore it is essential to discuss this because as parents we must recognize how this affects not just the emotions of our children but also their confidence, their self-awareness, and their futures. We have seen the fallouts—failing grades, angry demeanors, disruptive and sometimes aggressive behaviors. Children tend to act out their emptiness externally and young adults tend to internally crash. Most individuals who undergo divorce can speak of a sense of hitting an emotional rock bottom at the point of divorce. It is essential that they realize that so do their children. We all know there is a healthy and not-so-healthy way for man and wife to survive divorce; the same is true for each of the children. Just as the husband and wife must work through guilt, self-blame, grief, and anger, so does the child. Bottom line, as with economical bankruptcy two things can happen. One, you never regain your stability and struggle for the rest of your life. Or two, you use your time, talents, and sweat to rebuild and regain financial, spiritual, and emotional stability. I want to encourage you to choose the wise way so that you can assist your child with regaining their confidence, self-worth, and love for self and others. Parents will need to validate their children's feelings and allow them the opportunity to process everything either by talking, writing, or praying. If needed allow the child to have their own counselor as they rebuild their self-worth and confidence. Realize that their foundation for life has literally bottomed out, at least as far as they can see. Functionally a family unit brings quite the package. Father as the provider and protector, mother as the nurturer and organizer. When the family is functional everyone feels safe, secure, and they are productive and confident. When pieces are missing due to death, separation or divorce, everyone has to find their new comfort zone. Subsequently the entire family has to find their bearings and learn to stand tall again; this includes the parents and the children. Don't shun the children. Allow them to ask questions, to cry, and to reminisce. Don't erase or dismiss what they have experienced as normalcy their entire little lives. Be truthful with them, and if some information is too grown up let them know that will have to wait until they are older, or that is mommy and daddy's business. But do offer them explanations that are truthful and transparent. Ideally the parents would discuss what they will share and do it in two parts as a family. The initial announcement and then a follow-up discussion after the children have had an opportunity to process the "announcement." Last but certainly not least, don't bash. That is, don't speak negatively about your spouse in front of your children. Remember, children eventually grow up and they will make their own judgment call as to who behaved appropriately or not. Bashing can lead to your child feeling forced to choose one parent over another, which can literally rip their hearts apart.

Think about it. You loved your spouse for years and it likely took that long to fall out of love. We cannot expect our children to instantly fall out of love with the two people who made their lives possible, just because of a heartbreaking, disappointing "announcement." Can we really expect our babies to accept their entire lives changing just because of an announcement? Back to the bashing. Your ability to FORGIVE influences your ability to survive. Your survival increases your child's belief that they, too, will survive. The lack of forgiveness and continuous conflict sends a message of defeat to your child. Unforgiveness and bitterness translate to lifelong misery. It spreads a message of despair and may convince your child that it is impossible to survive setbacks in life. Divorce, whether we like it or not, is a family affair, and all entities need a safe environment to heal. I encourage parents to fill up on the Word of God so that you will not be emotionally and spiritually bankrupt during a time when your children so desperately need your wisdom, your guidance, and your best self as an example of how to survive adversity.

Bankruptcy by Abandonment

Abandonment and emotional bankruptcy are almost one and the same. One occurs when the parents' absence makes them unavailable, and the other when the parents' presence makes them unavailable. The former speaks for itself but let me expound on the latter. Imagine a parent, for example, with an addiction. If the parent's focus is on the drug, the child is rarely noticed and is rarely the focus. Imagine a parent with a severe mental illness. The parent's focus could be on their delusions and again the child is rarely seen, and the child's wants and needs unimportant. The bottom line here is a child can be abandoned in the absence and presence of a parent. This may lead to a needy child who acts out to gain attention; negative attention is better than none. This may lead to a child who becomes like a wallflower, unseen and unheard to minimize negative interactions. This may lead to teens who find themselves seeking confidence and love from all the wrong places—alcohol, drugs, sex, and delinquency. It is not my goal to reopen wounds for parents. However, the available parent must recognize that the unavailable parent is just as influential in the development of the child as the present parent. Ignoring only makes it that much more powerful and impactful, thus the reason we had to discuss it here. When a child is abandoned and have limited support emotionally, they will seek it wherever they can find it. The present parent can be a good source if they are not stuck in bitterness or so focused on themselves and their own needs that the child is pushed aside. If the present parent is healthy the child can get his or her needs met.

First and most important, be HONEST. Throughout the years this has arisen over and over as I work with families. Whether it is telling a child that he is adopted or telling them the truth about their missing parent, that day always comes. Truth is paramount; it cannot be hidden forever. Some details may need to be withheld until the child is at an age to understand, but the basic truth as soon as possible is crucial. The right age is right now, as soon as it crosses your mind, as soon as your child is asking questions. Concealing information and protecting secrets are a full-time job and next to impossible. Building your family's foundation on lies is a mountain slide waiting to happen. If counseling is necessary get it done. Whatever is necessary to get the truth on the table as soon as possible should be accomplished.

Children are very trusting and forgiving. The younger a child the more forgiving. Operating a family through lies is difficult to sustain. Besides how do we expect God to continuously bless our families when our foundation is built on lies?

So whether dealing with a serious illness, incarceration, drug addiction, or marital conflict, take the time to let your children know in the most nonjudgmental way possible the truth about their absent parent.

The next step is to find trusted surrogates. That is, if Dad is missing, make sure your child has healthy relationships with god-fearing uncles, grandfathers, or godfathers. Likewise if Mom is missing, aunts and grandmothers or godmothers. In the African American as well as many other cultures, this is one of the ways single parents can do so well: they utilize their village, whether extended family, community, or church to assist with rearing their children.

Bankruptcy by Death

This is a very familiar scene for me. God introduced me to compassion as a child, when my cousins lost their mother, my favorite aunt. We both had moles on our faces and she told me that was our beauty marks. I was in grade school. My heart would hurt for my cousins anytime someone asked why they were not living with their mother. I also watched my mother work tirelessly to assure that all six of the eight (the eldest was grown and the second oldest always lived with us) remained within the family, so sometimes my heart hurt for her as well. Subsequently I dedicated the first half of my private practice to treating and helping motherless children by working closely with child protective services and children under their guardianship. This went on for a season.

The most difficult emotion I observed from the many motherless children I worked with was embarrassment. It is almost like they feel responsible for the death of their mother. Let me share from my experience growing up. I can remember wanting to physically fight people who tried to force my cousins to tell them where their mother was. The pestering classmate would not have a clue of the emotions they were stirring up with their persistent inquiries. The tension in my mind was beyond what was necessary. I often thought to myself, *Leave her alone already. Enough is enough.* However, I would often be too angry to speak in a kind manner, so I remained quiet. The answer always came out with a sense of annoyance that they were forced to say it. "She's dead." I can still feel the pain stirred up when I hear those words. It is as if they brought my aunt alive with their words only to announce that she was dead once again. I am speaking of my emotional pain, and I am only the niece, so we can only try to empathize with the pain it stirred up in her children. What followed was remorse and pity, which did not feel any better.

Either way the child runs the risk of being emotionally bankrupt. How does this look, you may ask? Truthfully it depends on the child's personality, temperament, and connectedness with others. Overall this is a very sticky subject and multiple variables contribute to the final results. Each child is different and will respond differently, so this is just a few pointers to open our minds.

Love is key for motherless children. I don't believe anyone can love a child like their mother can; it is just impossible to completely emulate that bond. At any rate it is crucial that the surrogate mother try her best. I remember after we were all grown and one of my cousin/sisters, returned home from the military, where she had married and been exposed to her husband's family or perhaps others in the military. She told my mother and I, "We don't hug enough in this family. We need to do better." Wanda mentioning this was just enough to trigger more hugging. I say this because we must empower our children, especially our motherless children, to voice what they need. I have realized after rearing several boys and only two girls that most girls really need "a lot" of hugs. I should have known that from my childhood. Interestingly most of my hugs came from my daddy and my deceased aunt. Wow, I never realized that before now. My aunt Johnnie Mae (mother of the eight) was big on hugs. I say that to say my cousins, who came to live with me, were likely expecting the same from my mother, who was not a big hugger, until my cousin mentioned it and we were all grown then. As a result our children all received a zillion hugs from my mother during their time with "Granny," as she was called. My point here, once a child loses a parent, it is hard to know all the expressions of love that they were reared with that stopped instantly. It may be helpful to speak to the child about how love was expressed and what they miss most. A surrogate mother can teach a young girl how to be a lady, can love her, and protect her, but still may miss the mark because of the extras that their mother may have naturally offered. May I add that sometimes the child carries a demeanor which says "leave me alone." Especially early on after the death. This goes back to the foundational shift that comes with losing a parent. That foundation must be rebuilt, and the more solid, dependable, and lovable the surrogates are, the easier to rebuild the foundation, but it still takes time. I, as a habit, try to offer to as many young people as possible what I call "mommy hugs." I can remember when I would go to my son's football games, offering good ole fashion "mommy hugs" to as many of his teammates as possible, especially if their mothers lived far away.

I mentioned before, and it is crucial here as well, my husband's saying: "A mother rears her daughter and loves her son; a father rears a son and loves his daughter."

Thus, a son losing a mother can be just as difficult because the one person in the world who loves him, flaws and all, nonjudgmentally and unconditionally, is gone. Now he may feel he has no advocates left and will go through his life either trying to prove himself or giving up and not trying at all for fear of the rejection of his best not being enough.

If I may digress, this is the reason why an overbearing, critical wife can wear a man down. Men are hoping their marriage will recreate that bond of nonjudgmental and unconditional love, and when it does not they become very disengaged and eventually may even leave (more about that in the next book).

Back to the children. We must speak about a fatherless child. For a daughter, the father is her source of compliments, reassurance of her worth and beauty, as well as her protection. Predators look for this missing link to prey on young girls. It is essential that the present parent makes sure that the village around your child is of substance, godly, and ethical. Your village can make or break your child. Generational incest is avoidable. If they violated you, they will for sure attempt to violate your children. Govern yourself accordingly and please take the necessary precautions. Love from a distance with a watchful eye.

Bottom line, love, encourage, teach and live godly lives, and most definitely protect our children who have lost a parent. They are vulnerable and can easily be victimized. However, with the appropriate support, love, encouragement, prayers, and environment they can thrive.

For a son, his father is his example, his strength, his protection and sometimes linked to his purpose. A young son relies heavily on his mother but a teen to young adult son rely heavily on his father or a male role model. The absent father may dislodge the young man's sense of responsibility and purpose. From the teen years onward, the father is where the young man prefers to go for advice. The father is necessary to help shape his son and offer him clear guidance on transitioning into manhood. I must say that with the four young men we reared, once they reached age 21 it became obvious to me that my opinion was not desired. I could give them biblical guidance only, it appeared that most other statements were usually left on the table to be further discussed with their father. This did not upset me because they were all very respectful, but it was an observation that I noted and filed away.

Present Parent

For the parents who chose to not leave. Those who serve as co-parents or single parents. I want to share information to help you stay on your game. Most of this you already know, but I will use this catchy acronym to keep it simple and to the point. Families were designed by God to function with everyone staying in their roles. However, life can get rough and we find ourselves stressed and backed in a corner. I will describe the problem and then offer a solution, since this book is all about solutions.

When you are STRESSED every organ in your body is responding and often in an unhealthy manner. Our go-to for stress are DESSERTS. Yes, we just pile unhealthy on unhealthy. Please tell me you knew that STRESSED spelled backward is DESSERTS. If not, now you know. Most people don't know when they are stressed. If this is you, start paying attention to your body and the signs it gives you, to let you know you are overwhelmed.

S – SLEEP DISTURBANCE: too much or too little sleep or nightmares

T – THOUGHTS: scattered, negative, crowded, or hallucinating

R – RANTING: irritated and arguing with everyone

E – ENERGY: too low or too high

S – SADNESS: feeling down or crying a lot

S – SUICIDAL: no will to live, or entertain ideas of how to kill yourself

E – EMPTINESS: no hope, no self-worth, no help, and no excitement

D – DISCONNECTED: isolated, self-centered, or no concern for others

Let's talk solutions to the stress:

DESSERTS is our go-to, but try these desserts instead:

D – Doctor: that is who you want to see right away, if you are experiencing four or more symptoms of the stressed list above. WHY,

YOU ASK? Well, why do we take insulin for diabetes? To control our glucose. So why is it deemed ridiculous to take medications for depression? Stress expresses symptoms of either underlying anxiety or mood disorder. (True, it could also be other physical ailments such as thyroid, but right now we are speaking of our mental health.) That ability to live in harmony with our surroundings. Thus in this arena stress tells us that our brain neurotransmitters are not in harmony. Medications are sometimes necessary to get the brain back in check. (Commercial break: Xanax and Valium are not antidepressants but rather temporary Band-Aids for a wide-open wound.) Antidepressants can treat both anxiety and depression and they are not considered narcotics with addictive potential. The goal is to treat with the least amount of medication for a designated period to address a specific disorder. There are exceptions to this rule, but make sure a specialist is involved with the exceptions. Exceptions include treatment for recurrent or chronic conditions.

E – Exercise: walking, yoga, cycling, dancing, and the like. It helps relieve stress by driving your brains focus to your body rather than your emotions. Exercise can also release endorphins, which are the natural feel-good chemicals in your brain.

S – Spirituality: is there balance, do you know how to gain your inner peace? Meditation, prayer, and mindfulness help to clear your thoughts of negativity. This include forgiveness and living in harmony with self and others. (Dr. KSG tip: Clearing your mind is not emptying it but rather replacing negativity with positivity, truth, i.e. scriptures.)

S – Someone: spend time with someone positive who pours love and hope into you. Avoid those who take and take or who keep you feeling tensed due to their negativity.

E – Expand: your territory beyond YOU—reach out and help someone in worse shape than yourself. Service to others can improve your mood, redirect your anxiety, and extend the quality of your life.

R – Reach goals by setting them: daily, weekly, annually. Set goals for yourself and your family.

T – Try something new: step out of your comfort zone.

S – Start fresh: erasing the past, deciding to leave the baggage behind and start appreciating that the past is over, and guess what? You survived! Now let's thrive.

To add to our peace and less stress, lastly, I want to offer a few of Dr. KSG's parenting tips::

1) Never punish your children when you are angry.

2) Start each day fresh and new without any penalties from yesterday, especially with your young children ten and under.

3) Avoid long, drawn-out punishments that stress you and the child. Punishments should be a very specific duration with the parent, starting and ending it with an explanation of why the punishment was necessary. Time out, for example, can work but should be limited to a minute per year of age as a rule of thumb, for children under ten. Punishments for teens should last no more than a few days. Punishments only

work when the parent start and end them. If you forget or the child begs his way off the punishment—no healthy lesson is learned. Rather the child may learn to manipulate their way out of adversities, or that they do not have to finish anything.

4) Every child should feel the change in the atmosphere as a punishment starts and ends. A fresh start with no resentment is essential for a healthy punishment. New mercies every morning is promised by God (Lamentations 3:23). We should give our children the same courtesy.

5) Recognize when Mommy needs a time out and teach your children to give you a minute when you need it.

6) Parents try to avoid punishing by removing healthy groups or extracurricular activities that teens tend to enjoy. That is, if my child is acting out in class, I don't want to take them out of football where men are teaching structure, discipline, and hard work, leaving my child to spend their extra time with those teens uninvolved with school and doing nothing positive. If you want to utilize

the sports in punishment, go tell the coach the trouble you are having and allow them to incorporate the discipline in the healthy activity. Teens like groups and they will find one, whether healthy or not.

7) Remember that all that you do and say will become your legacy and repeated for generations, so take the time to think about the long-term effects of your actions and words on your children and grandchildren.

PART V

This section is personal. As I wrote this book for parents; it was indeed a sacrifice of my time but a joy to complete over the past two years. The thing about God, He is a "give and give" God, so of course as He gave me the stories and pointers to help you, He also gave me life lessons. In this section I will share my life lessons delivered only as a result of my obedience in completing this book. Sit back, relax, and enjoy the transparency and revelations of this author.

PART V

CHAPTER 11

PRAY BEFORE INVESTING

"Your calling massages your passion."
—Dr. KSG

In chapter 3, you read about my dream to reach my "ultimate goal" in life as a physician.

Even though I used that phrase—ultimate goal—for many years, I did not recognize that I had a calling related to it, until ten years after obtaining my ultimate goal. It was yet another ten years before I understood how to operate in my calling regarding the ultimate goal. You see, I always knew that I had compassion for others. I knew that compassion drew me to become a physician, but I did not know my passion.

I must share how God made this clear to me

because it was truly a process. It started... Brace yourself, with a very popular female-hosted talk show. You see, I am a hard-core kind of girl, reared in Kashmere Gardens, right next door to 5th Ward, Texas. So, I am not the cry-baby type. I am trained in Child and Adolescent Psychiatry, so I have heard the saddest stories and felt the deepest empathy and sympathy, but still no tears. Yet for years I could never understand why every time I saw a show where someone reached their ultimate goal, usually by financial or networking assistance, I would cry like a baby. I would pray and ask God why hearing these stories made me cry, when they were obviously happy occasions. I have heard that what moves you to tears is often your passion, so I really prayed and worked hard to figure this thing out. Initially I thought, *Well, is it the philanthropy portion? I am a giver, so maybe the giving moves me to tears.* So I told myself (yes, me, not the Holy Spirit), "I am a philanthropist at a smaller scale." (Kathy's economics). For the next ten-plus years, I found myself giving large and small amounts of money to almost anyone, requested or not, until one day my brother said to me, "Kathy, you are never going to have anything because you give too much away." Not long after that the IRS audited my husband and I because our giving was above the expected range for our income. I thought, *My brother is concerned about my personal giving and now the IRS is concerned about my charitable giving.* This propelled me into a whirlwind of prayer. I began to pray about my giving. God revealed to me that I was acting like a little "G," god. Rather than giving my recipients the opportunity to ask and rely on Him, they were coming to me. I also realized that I was often giving until it hurt my family financially. God did reveal to me that just because I had it, did not mean that I had it to give. To be transparent, this was pride. Giving because others expect it or because I could was not the giving that blessed God, nor that supported His economics for growth in His kingdom. Back to the drawing board, or should I say praying board. Since that revelation, I have learned to give only when prompted by the Holy Spirit, which has worked a lot better overall. By the time I realized that philanthropy was not my calling, my children were preteens. As a testament to God's economy, my obedience in when to give, led to God blessing both my husband and I with almost double the income we had the prior ten years, during my philanthropy season.

Today, another ten years later, my children are now grown. I now know that God gave me an extra dose of compassion to see others fulfill their ultimate dreams.

My tears for all those years the talk-show host delivered blessings to others were prayers of thanksgiving. I thanked God that I witnessed the recipient's satisfaction, their loved ones' appreciation, and the giver's joy as the blessing unfolded right before my eyes on national TV. I would cry, praising God for the blessing.

You see, it took thirty years for me to realize my calling regarding "ultimate goals." I finally understood my role in others' dreams as I completed an annual fast in January of 2016. That year, God insisted that I pray for my children's ultimate goals. He prepared me for even this task. First, I prayed for many years that I would reach my ultimate goal of becoming a physician. But in addition, annually for about ten years, during my January fast, I would ask my children to send their goals for the year so I could pray over them. To show them God's faithfulness, I would also share their prior year goals so they could see God's hand in their lives. Celebrating answered prayers and accomplishments was just as important as offering up the prayers. But the year 2016 was different. After my January fast, God placed it on my heart to pray for my children to reach their ultimate goals. This is a process, because there are seasonal goals that are stepping stones to gain the ultimate goal, and my young adults are still in seasons. When I started this book, only one really knew their ultimate goal. But as of today, after individually seeking God's will for their lives, all three at least know their ultimate goals. The point here is my learned lesson regarding my passion for others reaching their ultimate goals. It was not about what I could do or give them; it was always about me praying for the individual and allowing God to work out and order their steps. Finally, my assignment included making sure they knew God was behind the success and encouraging them to graciously give God the credit, praise, and glory.

This is the reason Uncle Edward's quote touched me so deeply. My calling is not based on what I offer or contribute. My calling is to pray for others to receive their ultimate goals, and boy when they do, what a time for celebration and praise to God for such an awesome blessing.

This thirty-year lesson has shown me how patient and amazing God is toward those whom He has called. I simply get to pray and then I get to shout and give God glory when He has brought all this to fruition for the individual. Lesson learned and now he blessed me to share this with you. Now I know why I often ask young people what their goals are. I may ask what they want to major in but follow up with, "So what do you want to do with that?" I now know that when they share especially specific goals, I must deliver a prayer on their behalf for their success. To summarize, our passions and callings are not always about doing something; sometimes it is about trusting Him to do it all. Praise break…

CHAPTER 12

HUGE MARGIN OF ERROR

"...I understood as a child, I thought as a child, but when I became a man, I put away childish things."(KJV)

—1 CORINTHIANS 13:11B

OK, so this chapter is a major self-revealing exercise for me, transparency and vulnerability at its best. The main message as per the title is to help us recognize that children don't always understand things the same as adults. The sad thing is, I don't know that there is anything magical, practical, or sensible we can do to change the huge margin of error in our children's miscalculations of some of the things they remember or interpret wrongly.

To illustrate this, let's go back to my mother praying Hannah's prayer to get her baby girl. I wonder if you noticed when this was discussed in chapter 7, I spoke of Samson in place of Samuel. The twist, or shall I say obstacle, for me was my confusion with relating my life to Samson rather than Samuel. As a five-year-old exploring and reading about Samson's life, getting the beautiful girl (Delilah), her cutting his hair and him defeating the Philistines single-handedly without the strength from his hair, yes, that had to be the greatest day of his life, and he died. Not soon after learning this story and having all my questions answered about my mother's prayer for a girl, I had a dream that shaped my life. At age five, I dreamt that God would take me back at my happiest moment. How scary is that? My fear thereafter was that literally, right in the middle of some grand celebration, I would disappear from the face of the earth and return to God. I literally lived my life discrediting every accomplishment as merely a stepping stone to something greater. For sure the day I married, had each of my children, and finished medical school, I thought I would just drop dead.

Fast forward about twenty-five years, during

the time I was writing this book, the Lord woke me up at 5 a.m. sharp one Friday morning, November 2017, for our time together. I had been reading the book of Judges which my husband suggested when I told him I wanted to focus on obedience. That Friday I started with chapter 11, and I literally stopped in my tracts in chapter 13. The story of Samson's birth is described there. They never mentioned his mother's name, only his father Manoah. Samson's mother was barren, but she did not pray for a son; angels appeared to tell her she was having a son. This instantly caught my attention. Yes, the angel spoke to her first and then the couple together to tell them the barren wife would have a son and that "no razor shall come upon his head and that he would deliver Israel out of the hand of the Philistines" (Judges 13:5).

That cool November morning, as I read this story, my lifelong fear was now a big question mark. I instantly searched my online Bible for Hannah, which of course took me to 1 Samuel chapter 1. Once I read that, I realized that a childhood memory with a huge margin of error had captivated and shaped a large component of my life.

Let me see if I can paint the picture of how my

mother's blessing and answered prayer became my worst nightmare. It all started with my mother trying to explain how blessed and wanted I was as a child. She and my father had all boys and she so desired a girl. So she prayed Hannah's prayer, desperately asking God for a girl, and she promised God that she would give me back to Him. This led to me searching the scriptures for my destiny. A five-year-old searching for Hannah's prayer was not very successful, so I asked my mother to read it to me. I remembered two things correctly from what she read: "That she would give her son back to God" and that "no razor would come upon his head" (1 Samuel 1:11). I remembered several things incorrectly, including the name, Samuel not Samson. But I also captured another memory of Eli's sons dying in their best days, which I thought was meant for me and Samson. (I Sam 2:33)

The part with no razor upon his head was a part of the Nazarene vow, described earlier, to which both Samuel and Samson were devoted. However, I did not know this as a child, so in my young mind, based on all the Bible stories I heard, this description pointed to Samson. Think about it. He is the one discussed in the children's Bible study books. He was the one with the long hair, betrayed by the lovely Delilah, the hero and the one who died early (in his best days or prime of his life). Therefore when I had my dream of dying at my happiest moment, it all again took me to Samson and led to the conclusion that I would die early doing something spectacular.

Look at Samson, born to destroy the Philistines, and he accomplished that, even if it was unto his death. To complete your purposed assignment on your dying bed, that had to be a happy or at least fulfilled day for him. For many years thereafter I expected something similar.

To add to this confusion, until the revelation above I could not for the life of me understand why my mother on her dying bed (October 2010) told me again that she prayed Hannah's prayer for me and she would be glad when I "step into my full potential." Now keep in mind, I was forty-nine years and eleven months old. I was a very successful child psychiatrist, well known in my community and even published in my field. I was married to an educator and minister with two Air Force academy students and a teen in the top one percent of his high school class. I was born again, saved, sanctified, and a teacher/speaker amongst Christian women and children. I have since pondered for many years what she meant by this, until that morning in November.

Once I searched Hannah's prayer and read about Samuel, I realized instantly how huge my margin of error was regarding my life and success. You see, Samuel had a very different life than Samson. A longer, more spiritually fruitful life. He was called very early by God and he used Samuel to speak to many on his behalf. He made disciples of many, including Saul, the first king of Israel. This epiphany may seem like yesterday's news to you, but it was huge for me and it opened my mind and path to soar. No longer did I have to ponder about Mother's last words. I could more clearly see that God wanted more for me and more from me.

God confirmed for me that he was pleased that I realized my life should be likened to Samuel rather than Samson by first the Sunday school lesson for that Sunday, which discussed Samuel's life versus Samson's, and simultaneously my Bob Gass Bible study book ran a five-day series, "Difference between Samson and Samuel."

This mistaken identity kept me humble, but I can only imagine the things I did not do for fear of this dream becoming a reality as well as the things I did do thinking I would die early. Now I know better, so I must do better. My life is not that of Samson's but of Samuel's, who was wise, a leader, and often made disciples of others and guided them into their potential in God, thus this book. What I now realize: a life of ministry rather than battles, a life of promise rather than demise, a life well and long lived rather than an abrupt sacrifice? Yes, Lord, I accept that correction and I am more than willing to make this major turn, to place my life on the right path! Praise break...

I share all of this to say that we never know how our words confuse our children. We rarely know what they are confused about. We don't always see what is driving them down the wrong path, but one thing we can all be sure of: God will straighten the crooked path to get them on track and He will do it right on time for His plan to come to fruition. So if you are a parent watching your child stray or go in the wrong direction or just operate beneath their potential, pray for them. Pray for their ability to reach their ultimate goals; pray for them to seek and trust God. Then know and believe that God will work it out for their good. Once again, God stepped in to turn my thinking toward his truth. Turning and re-turning throughout our lives is God's way.

CHAPTER 13

THE GREAT REWARD

"Trust in the LORD with all your heart, And
lean not on your own understanding; (NIV)
—PROVERBS 3:5

One final revelation regarding that life-altering
dream I had at age five. Let me remind you: I
dreamed that God would take me back at my happiest moment. How scary is that? Well, on April 24,
2018, as I reread this book from the beginning—as
I often did when I had not been writing for more
than a week—God revealed something to me about
this dream. In retrospect I believe that fear resided
in my subconscious for many years and through
many accomplishments. Then God revealed it to

me out of nowhere. The great reward for us as parents is seeing our children become successful. For some that has to do with careers, financial freedom, happy marriages, and strong families. For God success is accepting His plan of salvation, maturing in His Word, walking in His Spirit, and operating in His ordained purpose for our lives. This revealed to me what it means for God to take me at my happiest moment. My happiest moment is not about a specific accomplishment, but rather the completion of my God-given assignments here on earth. My happiest moment will begin when I reunite in the eternal heavens with my Savior and Lord, Jesus Christ. Of all the books I have read about heaven, from the Bible, especially Revelation 21 (one of my favorite), to *90 Minutes in Heaven* and the like, no one wants to return to this dying world once they experience the life and love of the truly joyous and magnificent heavens. We can only experience a limited happiness here on earth, but the happiness we experience when we reach glory will far surpass any happenstance on this earth. This removed all my fears. No more worries about God taking me on my happiest day, but rather joy in knowing what the song "Oh Happy Day" is all about. Thank you, Jesus, for revealing this to me on this day! Until then I will, with contentment, enjoy every emotion and experience you have for me on earth with my friends and loved ones. I wait with great joy for the "happiest day of my life," which my God ordained before I was formed in my mother's womb. Don't be confused. I am no different from you. I am not ready to go or leave earlier than God desires. However, I know that when he calls me I will go to heaven. This gives me peace. I know that I will experience a new form of happiness that is beyond my current capacity to imagine. I trust God.

PART VI

THE FINAL WORD

CHAPTER 14

THE GREAT PURCHASE

"For God so loved the world that he gave
His Only begotten Son that whosoever
believe in him shall not Perish but have
Everlasting Life."

—JOHN 3:16

ILLUSTRATION: DR. DAVID JEREMIAH

Over 2,000 years ago a plan for fallen man,
an opportunity for all human beings to be
returned to their rightful place in God's kingdom,
was established. This plan required time to materi-
alize. It was indeed a master's plan and every detail
had to be visited to assure success. This plan was
fail-proofed and had to be available to all man-
kind. This plan was a purchase, a Great Purchase.

135

Because of this purchase, today you and I can enjoy life and enjoy our families. This purchase was all inclusive and nonrefundable. This purchase allows us freedom to love and to live in harmony with one another, and freedom to live eternally in a much better place.

We are all accustomed to purchasing items we need: food, clothing, homes, cars, and so on. We offer currency to exchange for the item we want. There are some cultures that barter; they offer one item or service in exchange for another item or service. These purchases can be exchanged or refunded. But the "Great Purchase" works a little differently. First, the receiver does not have to give or sacrifice anything, so it is more like a gift. This purchase is somewhat one sided. The giver loses everything and the receiver gains everything. That sounds unfair, unrealistic, and unnatural. Indeed it is, because it is supernatural.

The Great Purchase can be best described by John 3:16: "For **God** so loved the world that he gave His **Only** begotten **Son** that whosoever believe in him shall not **Perish** but have Everlasting Life." As Dr. David Jeremiah illustrated in his book *God*

Loves You,[5] this one verse is the gospel, the great mystery, the good news, so much so that it even contains the word **GOSPEL**.

You see, we all owe God a debt because of our sin, and the only acceptable payment for sin is death—an eternal death (Romans 6:23a: "For the wages of sin is death..."). That always blows my mind. I can easily picture myself living forever, but to die forever sounds miserable. At any rate, God decided before we were even born that He would offer us the opportunity to choose an alternative to that punishment. Hallelujah!

Option 1: Remain a sinner and choose eternal death

Option 2: Choose His Son as Savior and be saved from eternal death

Option 2 is possible because Christ paid for all our sins by dying in our place. The beauty is that He rose again, which assures us that we will live forever just as Christ lives.

---

[5] *God Loves You* by Dr. David Jeremiah, Faith Words 2012. Page 118.

Any who does not choose Option 2 automatically defaults to Option 1. Option 2 requires a conscious decision of accepting John 3:16:

- I believe that Jesus is God's Son born through the virgin Mary. (Matthew 1:23)
- I believe He is without sin. (Hebrews 4:15)
- I believe He took on not just my sins, but all the sins of the world, on the cross with Him where He died. (II Corin 5:21; Philippians 2:8)
- I believe He remained dead for three days and rose on the third day with all power in heaven and earth. (Mark 16:6; Romans 14:9; I Peter:22)
- I believe He is now sitting at the right hand of God. (1 Peter 3:22)
- I believe He is advocating for me and reminding the accuser that He has already paid for my sins via the Great Purchase. (Romans 8:34)
- It is that simple, and all you must do is BELIEVE. (Romans 10:9; Luke 23:42-43)

So many try to complicate salvation, but if you read in Luke 23, when Christ was hanging on the cross between the two thieves, you will see the simplicity. One thief ridiculed Christ but the other reprimanded him, stating, and I will paraphrase, "The two of us are crooks and we deserve this death (confession), but He is innocent (recognizing him as sinless and therefore God) and dying for no wrongdoing (not his sin but the sin of the world)." Jesus then stated to him, "Today you will be with me in paradise" (Luke 23:43) (Salvation). Salvation is not complicated and there are no hoops to jump through. It is believing and receiving the greatest gift known to man, Jesus Christ as your Savior.

Yes, Jesus purchased all my sins with the blood He shed on the cross. This purchase paid the debt for all my sins and yours; therefore I will not enter the gates of hell. Yes, my flight to heaven is paid in full.

The Great Purchase offers many benefits, not just eternal life, not just escaping eternal death, but that day on the cross several things happened that benefit those who accept Jesus as their Savior. Jesus shed blood to pay for our sins, and He shed water from His pierced side, which cleanses us of all unrighteousness. Therefore we can live without being slaves to sin. We will have no condemnation (no death) for our sins (Romans 8:1). That same day the veils in the temple were torn (Luke 23:45). We then had a direct connection to God's power, His love, the fruit of His spirit, and a direct line of communication with a Holy God through prayer. All of this and more, because of the Great Purchase. As we make decisions to reduce the challenges that come with rearing children, introducing them to the benefits of the Great Purchase appear to be a strategy to promote success, safety, and security.

CHAPTER 15

CONCLUSION

It is so God to have revealed something new to me about myself as I wrote this book. For all I know, those revelations for me may have been the whole purpose for me writing it, thereby leaving me with a stack of books that never sell. That is fine, and if that is God's will I have a large stack of shower gifts, and Christmas and birthday gifts for all the young parents I know. If you did purchase it, I truly appreciate it and will make sure that at least ten percent is used to bless families. At any rate it excites me to think of what is next, not just for you and your children, but for me and mine. We are all His children and His economics apply to each of us. Whatever we invest our time, energy, and finances in will deliver some type of results.

Why take the risk in investing in something that is not proven when we have the opportunity to invest in something that will more than double our return? God has been proven over and over in the Bible and over and over in each of our lives. Parenting is no different. If we pour in the world, we will get the world. But if we pour in the Word, our return will be more than we could think or ask. This book is just one example of how consistent God is. The Bible is the original source for all of God's promises and consistencies. Jesus Christ is the same yesterday, today, and forever (Hebrews 13:8). There are no moving variables with Him. If we could minimize all of our margins of error, we could enjoy so much more of His benefits. That is, we as His children must read and judge our thoughts, memories, and beliefs based on His Word. My margins of error have likely delayed my ministry work. What is strange is I have read Samuel before, but Judges was not a book I read previously. This oversight has now been brought from my hindsight to my complete focus. A valuable lesson learned, we need to read the entire Bible over and over, as my husband has suggested, from front to back, numerous times and watch God's revelations. I encourage you to do as Deuteronomy 6 tells us. Love him, know him, and teach him so that you and your descendants can live long and prosperous lives as per God's economy.

It is my prayer that this pouring out of my experience as a mother will bless you and your children to operate in the knowledge of God, so that your dividends will be loaded with blessings and your spirit will line up with God's Word.

My last lesson came the very night I was scheduled to finalize this book before turning it over to my editors. So like God. He kept saying to finish the book, so that week I fast and prayed but observed that most of my praying was for others, not myself and the book. Amazingly the night I finished the book, I received a call and He revealed my next assignment. For years I have worked to live up to a claim I made on national TV, describing myself as the "praying sister" on the Today Show (Oct. 2, 2014) with my friend Toni and my sister-in-law Cheryl, both breast cancer survivors. At any rate, at the end of a very long workday, I received a call and was asked to be the Chaplain for a local graduate Chapter, of my sorority. Well, I did not have to pray about this one. Wow, God! If you are looking for me, I will be offering prayers for over 500 of my sorority sisters. Thanking God for bringing to fruition my claim of being "the praying sister", I humbly accepted this major role. God just keeps turning and re-turning. Thank you, God. Excuse me for this final praise break...

The end!

APPENDIX

Appendix 1

"Measure of a Man"
By: Rev. Edward L. Gurnell, D.D.

Not — "How did he die?"
But — "How did he live?"
Not — "What did he gain?"
But — "What did he give?"
These are the units
To measure the worth
Of a man, as a man,
Regardless of birth.
Not — "What was his station?"
But — "Had he a heart?"
And — "How did he play
His God-given part?
Was he ever ready
With a word of good cheer,

To bring back a smile.
To banish a tear?"
Not — "What was his church?"
Not — " What was his creed?"
But — "Had he befriended
Those really in need?"
Not — "What did the sketch
In the newspaper say?"
But — "How many were sorry
When he passed away?"

Appendix 2

Erikson's Stages of Psychosocial Development

Approximate Age	Psycho Social Crisis
Infancy - 18 months	Trust vs. Mistrust
18 months - 3 years	Autonomy vs. Shame and Doubt
3 - 5 years	Initiative vs. Guilt
5 - 13 years	Industry vs. Inferiority
13 - 21 years	Identity vs. Role confusion
21 - 39 years	Intimacy vs. Isolation
40 - 65 years	Generativity vs. Stagnation
65 and older	Ego Integrity vs. Despair

3/31/19

https://www.bing.com/images/search?q=Erikson%27s+
Stages+of+Development&FORM=RESTAB

Appendix 3

Quotes

1. "God's economics are fail-proof." —Dr. KSG
2. "Man's economy (give and take) versus God's economy (give and give)." —Dr. KSG
3. "A man's success is not measured by what he does or gains in life, but by the success of his children." —Uncle Edward Gurnell
4. "Be honest, are you living a life worth repeating?" —Dr. KSG
5. "Legacy, the gift that keeps giving". —Dr.KSG
6. "Life lessons sometimes come in small packages." —Dr. KSG
7. "A mother loves her son and rears her daughter and a father loves his daughter and rears his son."—Morris V. Gurnell, Jr

8. "Behold, children are a gift of the LORD, The fruit of the womb is a reward. Psalms 127:3 (NASB)

9. "For by your standard of measure it will be measured to you in return." —Luke 6:38b (NASB)

10. "Love with forgiveness heals all brokenness." —Dr. KSG

11 "Emptiness drains possibilities."—Dr. KSG

12 "Your calling massages your passion." —Dr. KSG

13 "...I understood as a child, I thought as a child, but when I became a man, I put away childish things." —1 Corinthians 13:11b, (KJV)

14. "Trust in the LORD with all your heart, and lean not on your own understanding;" Proverbs 3:5 (NKJV)

15. "For **God** so loved the world that he gave His **Only** begotten **Son** that whosoever believe in him shall not **Perish** but have **Everlasting Life**." —John 3:16, KJV Illustration: Dr. David Jeremiah

CPSIA information can be obtained
at www.ICGtesting.com
Printed in the USA
LVHW090347031019
633029LV00001B/4/P

9 781400 326051